Avoiding the 12 Relationship Mistakes Women Make
Georgia Shaffer

Seriously, how does she do that? How does Georgia Shaffer *so* completely nail those incredibly important relationship issues we so easily miss? Even better, Georgia's clear, practical, and beautifully biblical helps are spot-on for not simply identifying the obstacles, but for bringing us to the place of breakthrough—and bringing us to that sweet place of making better, wiser, God-honoring decisions. This is life-changing stuff!

Rhonda Rhea, author of 12 books,
including *Espresso Your Faith* and *Get a Grip*

If I had read this book as a young woman I would have avoided so many mistakes that took years to unravel. Georgia does a masterful job of dissecting the relational mistakes we make and building a bridge to looking at ourselves authentically. Through this authenticity we are free to break away from guilt, pain, and shame and live in the relational freedom God intends for us.

Gari Meacham, international speaker
and author of *Spirit Hunger* and *Truly Fed*

Staying on course in relationships will be easier than ever with your own relationship GPS system, as author **Georgia "Powerful" Shaffer** delivers spot-on direction once again with her advice to help women avoid serious relationship mistakes. *Avoiding the 12 Relationship Mistakes Women Make* is an indispensable companion for the journey.

Allison Bottke, author of the Setting Boundaries® series.

Every high school should issue incoming freshmen with a copy of *Avoiding the 12 Relationship Mistakes Women Make*, but if your school fell down on the job, it's not too late. I'm buying a copy for each of my daughters and enough extras to pass out to all my friends who can't understand why they just can't get this "friend thing" figured out. Because of this book, there are going to be a lot more women who are making the right relationships work.

Kathi Lipp, author of *The Husband Project*

If you are ready to recognize your relational blind spots and move forward into a brighter future, you're holding the right book. Like a cool big sister teaching you how to drive, Georgia shows you the clear path toward peace and fulfillment in your most important relationships.

Shannon Ethridge, author of the Every Woman's Battle series

Georgia's book is like having 12 sessions with a personal counselor. Writing with vulnerability about her own experiences, Georgia shares principles of healthy relationships and what we need to do to achieve them. If you want to understand yourself and others more fully, read this.

Poppy Smith, International Speaker, Author, Spiritual Life Coach

Relationship expert and life coach, Georgia Shaffer, skillfully and tenderly opens our eyes to potential blind spots in our closest relationships. With scriptural insight, thought-provoking instruction, and practical application steps, Georgia shows us how to avoid destructive interactions and be better equipped to enjoy healthier, more fulfilling relationships.

Sharon Jaynes, author of *The Power of a Woman's Words*

We all have relationship blind spots and Georgia Shaffer's book will help you develop good "I" sight. This book will help you see clearly and make good choices.

Linda Mintle, author of *Letting Go of Worry*

Are you a woman who is sick and tired and stuck when it comes to enjoying a successful and satisfying relationship? If so, Georgia Shaffer gives advice, encouragement, and spiritual inspiration to help you pinpoint what you're doing that doesn't work and what to do to make it work.

Karen O'Connor, author of *When God Answers Your Prayers*

Revealing and honest, Georgia tenderly unveils the many layers of relationship mistakes that we make. In working through this book, I asked God to gently guide me to truth and He did. I found it to be freeing and strengthening, even though at times it was difficult and made me uncomfortable with myself. I experienced a tremendous amount of life-giving application and healing in this process. I highly recommend this book for any woman of any age.

Janette Felder, Women's Ministry Events Director Ada Bible Church

This is such a helpful and thought-provoking book. The tips were fantastic. I got insights, slaps in the face, and *oh, wows*! all the way through the book. God has gifted Georgia with great insight and the ability to express it well in writing. You'll want to get this book and devour it!

Deb Haggerty, Certified Habits of Health Coach, Plymouth, MA.

Avoiding the 12 Relationship Mistakes Woman Make

GEORGIA SHAFFER

HARVEST HOUSE PUBLISHERS
EUGENE, OREGON

Cover by Left Coast Design, Portland, Oregon

Published in association with the Books & Such Literary Agency, 52 Mission Circle, Suite 122, PMB 170, Santa Rosa, CA 95409-5370, www.booksandsuch.com.

Cover photo © Matthew Williams-Ellis / Shutterstock

Names and minor details have been changed in the real-life stories shared in this book to protect the privacy of the individuals mentioned.

AVOIDING THE 12 RELATIONSHIP MISTAKES WOMEN MAKE
Copyright © 2014 by Georgia Shaffer
Published by Harvest House Publishers
Eugene, Oregon 97402
www.harvesthousepublishers.com

Library of Congress Cataloging-in-Publication Data
Shaffer, Georgia.
Avoiding the 12 relationship mistakes women make / Georgia Shaffer.
    pages cm
ISBN 978-0-7369-4934-7 (pbk.)
ISBN 978-0-7369-4935-4 (eBook)
1. Interpersonal relations—Religious aspects—Christianity. 2. Women—Psychology. I. Title. II. Title: Avoiding the twelve relationship mistakes women make.
BV4597.52.S53 2014
248.8'43—dc23

2013022892

Printed in the United States of America

13 14 15 16 17 18 19 20 21 22 / VP-JH / 10 9 8 7 6 5 4 3 2 1

With love and appreciation to my truth-tellers:
Kyle, Ron, Gayle, and Linda.

You know me best and love me enough
to help me see what it is I do not see.

Acknowledgments

It is a real joy to show my appreciation to those who helped make this book possible.

I'm especially grateful for those who prayed, shared their insights and wisdom, and encouraged me throughout this project: my mother, the Lancaster Writer's Group, Linda Jewell, Ron Hershberger, Penny Olivieri, Diane Pestes, Gayle Roper, Sue Smith, Leslie Vernick, and Deb Strubel for her editorial suggestions and support.

A special thanks goes to Janet Kobobel Grant, my literary agent, and Kathleen Kerr at Harvest House Publishers.

Contents

able to make the necessary adjustments because we think we are able to see ourselves and others clearly. We are *most* vulnerable to the negative impact of our blind spots when we ignore their existence.

We think we can see what others fail to notice, yet at the same time we fail to pay attention to our own blindness. As Jesus said, "Why do you look at the speck of sawdust in your brother's eye and pay no attention to the plank in your own eye?" (Matthew 7:3). As social psychologists and authors Carol Tavris and Elliot Aronson say, we are "as unaware of our blind spots as fish are unaware of the water they swim in."[1]

They write, "The brain is designed with blind spots, optical and psychological, and one of its cleverest tricks is to confer on us the comforting delusion that we, personally, do not have any." Our brains are wired in such a way that they allow "us to justify our own perceptions and beliefs as being accurate, realistic, and unbiased. We assume that other reasonable people see things the same way we do. If they disagree with us, they obviously aren't seeing clearly."[2]

Without an awareness of our relational blind spots, we can keep repeating the same mistakes over again. When we grow in self-awareness, however, we're able to remove many of the obstacles that hinder our growth. As a result, we'll resolve conflicts in a constructive way and deepen our closest connections. We'll be able to enjoy the kind of relationships we really want.

In the following chapters we'll discuss twelve relational blind spots. We'll learn how they sabotage our relationships and discuss specific strategies to avoid their destructive impact. To help you see what you may not be seeing, each chapter concludes with "Stop: Proceed with Caution" questions. You can use these questions for a small group study or on your own. I encourage you to write the first thing that comes to your mind as you answer the questions.

We each have learned through our own experiences that as intelligent people we can do some pretty stupid things. Be willing to gain the insights needed to grow in self-awareness and see yourself truthfully. Then you'll be able to say, "I was blind but now I see!"

How to S.P.O.T. What You Have Not Seen

If you were taught to drive many years ago, you might not be aware that you have two visual blind spots in front of you when driving. These blind spots are the result of the frame supporting the front windshield. Unless you keep your eyes on the road while also shifting the position of your head forward or backward, a pedestrian, truck, or another car can disappear behind that frame. Not only can we not see what's hidden behind that frame, but our brains think we see the whole road even though our vision is blocked. This is because our brains naturally fill in any gaps in our field of vision.

I know a man who hit a woman crossing the street because she happened to be hidden behind the frame on the right side of his windshield. The upset driver kept repeating, "I didn't see her." Likewise, in relationships, you need to intentionally employ strategies to discern when a blind spot could be sabotaging you.

In order to experience those all-important breakthroughs, here are four key ways to S.P.O.T. what you may not be seeing:

Seek God's wisdom
Pause for clarity
Open yourself up to wise counsel
Take a step back to gain a new perspective

Seek God's Wisdom

One of my coaching clients recently realized that when she runs into a problem or conflict at home or at work, she will first call her closest friend or Google the issue. Sometimes she'll solicit the opinions of her coworkers. She only begins to pray about the problem when she can't find a solution. She said, "I just realized as I'm talking to you that when I do start praying, that's usually when I experience a major breakthrough. Why didn't I realize that before?" Like many of us growing up, she wasn't trained to first seek the wisdom of God. Even though she has become a Christian, she continues to fall back on patterns and habits she had formed years ago.

Jesus warned his disciples about people who don't seek his truth and wisdom: "Though seeing, they do not see; though hearing, they do not hear or understand" (Matthew 13:13). In contrast, the disciples did search for the things of God and because of this Jesus said to them, "Blessed are your eyes because they see, and your ears because they hear" (Matthew 13:16). Like the disciples, in order to have eyes that see, we need to pray that the Holy Spirit, the Spirit of truth, will guide us and show us what we might be missing. As Henry Blackaby and Claude King write, "God speaks by the Holy Spirit through the Bible, prayer, circumstances and the church to reveal Himself, His purposes, and, His ways." [3]

If you are seeking God's wisdom through Scripture, it's important to read it regularly. As you read, ask God to reveal areas of blindness by asking questions like the following:

- What do You want me to see?
- Which of my motives have I been blind to?
- How have I been judgmental of others?
- What negative emotions am I harboring?

When seeking God's wisdom through prayer, don't forget that an important part of communication is listening to what He is saying. To help me remember and stay focused on what I believe God is telling me, I record what I hear in my journal. When I fail to write down what I'm hearing, it's frightening how quickly I forget what He has pointed out through Scripture or through His quiet whispers. He promises, "I will guide you along the best pathway for your life. I will advise you and watch over you" (Psalm 32:8 NLT).

When we get in the habit of paying attention and listening to God, we gain confidence in knowing that we really can communicate with him. As Henri Nouwen once wrote, "God is a God of the Present and reveals to those who are willing to listen carefully...the steps they are to take toward the future." [4]

Last year, in the midst of a hectic season, I received a call to speak at an event just a few weeks away. Everything in me wanted to say no. I wanted to tell this person I was tired and I needed some downtime to recharge. But I immediately thought, *Georgia, it's not about you. What does God want me to do?* I asked for a day to pray about it and the orga-nizer graciously gave me several. I asked two friends to pray with me for clarity and one said, "You do have a lot to offer on this topic."

It wasn't until the day I needed to give an answer that I had the impression I was not to speak at the event and would be disobedient if I accepted the invitation. Even though I didn't expect that answer from God, I sent an email to the event planner saying I was sorry but I would not be able to speak.

A month later, when I heard the speaker deliver a powerful pre-sentation, I knew I had heard God correctly. The experience really boosted my confidence in my ability to hear His still, small voice. It also reminded me that if I'm not listening to Him I can get in the way of what He has planned not only for me but for others.

When you just aren't sure what God wants for you, continue to pray and listen. I especially like what Oswald Chambers has written about discerning if what we are hearing is of God. He writes, "I know when the instructions have come from God because of their quiet per-sistence." [5]

Whether you feel it once or repeatedly, you don't want to ignore God's consistent gentle tap on your shoulder.

Pause for Clarity

Another strategy for uncovering what you're missing is to pause and give yourself plenty of time to gain clarity.

Pat, who is in my writer's critique group, shared a recent experience with me. "One morning I stopped at the end of my driveway before pulling out on the main road. I looked to my left and then to my right. I even double-checked, looking to my left and right a second time. As I slowly pulled out, an Amish horse and a buggy seemed to come out of nowhere. I hit the brakes and realized they had been perfectly posi-tioned not only behind the windshield frame to my right but also had disappeared behind the cherry tree on the right side of the driveway."

A horse and a buggy aren't as long as a tractor trailer, but they are still long. Yet they were both hidden from her view by two different obstructions. As is typical of our blind spots, she did not know her view was blocked. Thankfully, double-checking and carefully pulling out enabled her to avoid a collision.

Harvard psychologist David Perkins discovered through his research that we don't always recognize when it is a good time to stop and think. Yet these "thinking opportunities," as he calls them, are crucial to making intelligent choices. [6] In one study he found that a lack of sensitivity to thinking opportunities could have been "a *greater barrier* to intelligent behavior than either lack of motivation or limited ability." [7]

Of course there are times when you have to make an immediate decision and don't have the luxury of waiting. When time does permit, however, be willing to pause. Gather the facts or the insights needed for making good choices. Pause to pray. Pause to ponder. Pause so you can avoid the pitfalls. "The plans of the diligent lead to profit as surely as haste leads to poverty" (Proverbs 21:5).

Open Yourself Up to Wise Counsel

What's especially fascinating about our relational mistakes is that even though we don't see our own situations clearly, we often see others' circumstances accurately. This means other people may have a better understanding of what's going on in your relationships than you do.

I'm sure you have made a comment or heard someone say, "I can't believe she doesn't see how deceptive her husband is!"

"Why can't she see how hurtful her comment was?"

"When will she realize her friend is only manipulating the situation?"

Since you can easily miss what is obvious to others, wise counsel is helpful to correct any misperceptions or help you see a situation from a different angle. Have you ever been backing up in your car when someone says, "Stop! There's a car behind us." Don't you appreciate that kind of advice? Aren't you relieved to know you've just avoided an accident that would have been your fault?

In the same way, don't be too quick to discount the suggestions of those who ride through life with you. It may seem like your family, close friends, or coworkers are being overprotective at times, but their viewpoints could help you avoid unnecessary hurt and harm—a relational wreck. At least be willing to hear what they have to say and pray about it.

If you don't have a trusting truth-teller in your life, reach out to someone you respect and begin to build an honest friendship. Then don't be afraid to ask if they see something you aren't noticing in yourself or in your relationships.

Years ago I worked with a woman whom I believed to be my friend. I'll call her Sara. I would sometimes be wounded or discouraged by Sara's critical comments, but I honestly thought she was telling me those things because she wanted what was best for me.

One day another coworker, Kate, whom I respected, witnessed Sara throwing a sarcastic jab my way. Seeing how discouraged I was Kate later said, "Georgia, when are you going to realize Sara really isn't your friend? Can't you see how jealous she is of you? She takes a little bit of truth and then tries to destroy you with it."

I realized Kate was right. As I thought over my recent interactions with Sara, I could see how my supposedly supportive friend had been slowly undermining my confidence. Kate helped me remove my blinders. I was no longer deluded about Sara's motives, which I had failed to identify on my own.

On a different occasion, however, Kate gently pointed out to me that she thought I was having problems admitting I was wrong. She was right again. I was struggling to apologize to a different coworker. But because Kate spoke the truth in a respectful manner, I knew she was not trying to shame me. Not only did I appreciate her honesty, but I sought Kate's perspective more frequently after that, knowing she could be trusted to tell me what I needed to hear.

Proverbs reminds us it is the wise person who is willing to be corrected. "If you listen to constructive criticism, you will be at home among the wise" (Proverbs 15:31 NLT). Are you willing to ask for a gentle correction? Do you have at least one truth-teller in your life? Someone who will tell you what you need to hear without belittling you? You probably know people like Sara who wound you in the process of twisting the truth. Find people like Kate who will encourage you and challenge you to grow.

While it's important to be open-minded enough to hear the perspectives of others, be careful how much power you give to one person's opinion. Does this person share your values? Have they shown over time that they have your best interest in mind? Or do they have a hidden motive or a vested interest in looking at your situation in a certain way?

Nikki was engaged to be married in six months. She had this nagging feeling that she should not go forward with the wedding because her fiancé seemed to be drinking more and more. She shared her concerns with her parents and her pastor. Everyone assured her she was just having a case of cold feet. Her mother told her, "It's normal to feel that way. Don't worry. It will all work out."

Nikki has now been divorced for two years and still wonders, "Why didn't I pay more attention to my gut instincts? I knew it wasn't going to work. I think my parents had so much financially invested with the gown and the deposit for the reception and flowers they weren't willing to look at my concerns. As for my pastor, he probably wasn't around my fiancé and me long enough to understand what was going on."

When I asked Nikki what she would do differently, she said, "Looking back I realize I never prayed about my decision. At that time in my life I didn't know how to seek God's wisdom."

Seeking the counsel of wise people is important. But when it's combined with prayer, reading Scripture, and waiting for God's direction, we'll have a much greater chance of seeing the situation clearly.

Take a Step Back to Gain a New Perspective

Relationships are riddled with misperceptions, misunderstandings, and conflict. We tend to be shortsighted, seeing only our hurts and wounds and discounting the pain of others. "Pain felt is always more intense than pain inflicted." [8]

So how do you as a flawed person relating to imperfect people minimize the relational fallout you endure? How can you gain a new perspective and look at a situation with fresh new eyes? Seeing the big picture isn't always easy, but here are some suggestions to get you started.

First, *break away.* Walking away from a heated discussion not only defuses intense interactions, but it can give you a chance to allow the rational part of your brain to kick in. Taking a day trip, investing in a retreat, or going on a vacation isn't always feasible, but these getaways from your normal schedule and worries can be invaluable in gaining the mental and emotional distance you sometimes need. As author Mark Batterson suggests, "Sometimes you have to get out of your routine so God can speak to you in a non-routine way."[9]

Second, *brainstorm with someone.* One of the benefits of working with a coach or counselor is brainstorming the many different options or ways you can approach a task or a relational problem. You don't need to seek professional advice if you have a neighbor or friend who is talented in reframing issues. The problem is that sometimes, like you, they might not be objective enough either.

Finally, *balance the perceptions.* When you are hurt, offended, or misunderstood, try to see the situation from another person's perspective. What are they feeling? How are they viewing what happened? Sometimes it is too painful to discuss situations immediately and sometimes it isn't safe to revisit a conversation. But in general, you can gain insight from taking some time to clarify past interactions. This is far better than tending a wound for years.

When you want to gain some distance and see the bigger picture, breaking away, brainstorming, and balancing your perceptions can be helpful, but these are not the only approaches you can use. What have you found that works to help you reframe your situation?

We've addressed a few strategies to S.P.O.T. what it is you've failed to notice. In the next twelve chapters, we'll discuss each of the relationship mistakes in detail and give you practical suggestions for overcoming them. Remember: Growing in self-awareness is essential to building strong healthy relationships.

STOP: **Proceed with Caution**

Your answers to these questions will help you identify and learn to see what it is you are not seeing. In a journal, write down the first thing that comes to your mind.

1. What is your first reaction when you are struggling with a relational issue? Do you pray? Seek the advice of a friend? Search the Internet? Talk to a neighbor or coworker?

2. Are you comfortable asking a few wise people if they see something you're failing to notice? If you are hesitant, what are your concerns?

3. In the book of James we read, "If any of you lacks wisdom, you should ask God, who gives generously to all without finding fault, and it will be given to you" (James 1:5). If you are having problems with someone in your life and feel you could use more wisdom dealing with it, write a prayer asking the Holy Spirit for discernment.

1

I Don't See Myself As I Really Am

I protect myself by refusing to know myself.
FLORIANO MARTINS

Did you know you can buy blind-spot mirrors for your car? These mirrors are placed on the outside corner of your side-view mirror. It takes a special mirror for us to gain an accurate awareness of what's around us. This knowledge, in turn, helps us to avoid sideswiping another car.

Wouldn't it be helpful if there were a blind-spot mirror that enabled you to accurately see what's in your heart and mind? Then, with a little adjustment of your mirror, you could see what you failed to notice earlier and avoid sideswiping those who cross your path.

Then again, maybe you feel more like my friend who said, "Some days I really don't want an objective view of myself." She recognizes how uncomfortable it can be when some of her self-perceptions are shattered. She's experienced the pain that comes with a clear understanding of the undesirable ways she sometimes affects others.

Failing to see ourselves accurately is the first relationship mistake we are going to discuss in detail. Recently I was waiting in a checkout line and overheard the two women in front of me talking about a mutual acquaintance. One said, "I agree. She is always so down on herself. She is such a lovely supportive friend. I wish she could see herself as we see her—genuine and caring."

Sometimes, like the woman they were discussing, growing in self-awareness means to acknowledge, appreciate, and be willing to share the strengths and gifts we possess. Seeing ourselves accurately, however, also includes recognizing and accepting our flaws.

Because lack of self-awareness causes us to relate with others in all kinds of painful or unhealthy ways, growing in this area is crucial. Our self-awareness impacts every aspect of our lives, including how well we perform our jobs. For example, research has found that in a work setting 83 percent of the top performers rate high in self-awareness while only 2 percent of bottom performers do.[1] Some characteristics of those with an accurate view of themselves include

- clarity about what they do well and how they can help others
- aware of their flaws and hidden motives
- willing to spend the time needed for self-reflection
- recognize emotional triggers
- open to learning from their mistakes

While seeing our true nature doesn't always prevent us from hurting others, it does enable us to be more sensitive to the ways we can grow and gain true humility. One of my coaching clients, Macy, has a high level of self-awareness and recently struggled with what she described as "an ugly part of myself." As president of a consulting company, she recently lost a quarter-of-a-million-dollar contract she was sure she would get. She discovered that she was not merely disappointed but *devastated* at the loss of potential income. She prayerfully took time to reflect on what happened and her over-the-top reaction to it.

During our coaching session she said, "I did not want to share with you the unflattering way I handled this whole situation. But I knew if I was to grow, I had to be honest with God, myself, and you."

Macy realized she had been overconfident and made a few mistakes and misjudgments along the way. "What bothers me the most, though, is I didn't realize how focused I was on the money. Instead of caring for my client's needs I kept thinking about how landing this large contract would get me out of debt. It was all about me and the money.

"That's not how I built my business. My customers were a priority," she said. "I can't believe how quickly I abandoned my values and made an idol out of money."

Macy was quite down about herself and came close to landing in the pit of despair and self-loathing. Troubling thoughts threatened to consume her. Thoughts like, "You're a fake. You really don't care about people. It's all about you." Instead of pushing away the pain of seeing her uncaring behavior, she admitted her poor choices, recognized the condemning voice of Satan, and sought to refocus on God and others.

One of the main hazards of seeing ourselves accurately is getting stuck in our guilt, pain, and shame. I was reminded of this truth recently when someone I never met before told me how inconsiderate she thought I was of other people. On this particular morning I had taken my mother to a specialist for a medical procedure that included anesthesia. My mother lives in an assisted-living facility and has a handicapped parking placard that her drivers can place on the dashboard. When my mother is with me, I look for handicapped parking places. It's a habit. On the way back to her home, Mother asked me to stop at a grocery store to buy some small containers of Jell-O and applesauce. Her stomach was upset, and she thought that was about all she could eat. As I pulled into the handicapped parking place, I told her I would dash into the store alone and get those items.

As I walked from my car to the main entrance, a woman came up to me and said, "I just want you to know I don't appreciate the fact that you parked in that handicapped spot when you clearly have no problems walking."

I started to defend myself. "My mom just had surgery. We've been up since 4:00 this morning and it has been a long, difficult week. I've been using handicapped spots all morning. I just absentmindedly pulled into that spot not considering that my mom wasn't getting out of the car at this stop." But I stopped my defense. She was right and I knew it. I hadn't thought of other people when I pulled into that parking place. It was embarrassing to have it pointed out so publicly.

I felt like someone had just kicked me in the stomach. My prideful self-image had been shattered. The rest of the day I kept beating myself up about my uncaring behavior. When we catch glimpses of the unflattering parts of ourselves, it's emotionally distressing. At times like that we have a choice. We can rationalize our behavior and make all kinds of excuses about why we did what we did. We can blame others. We can even choose to believe the lies the evil one tells us about who we are. Or we can embrace the pain of being exposed and admit that we are flawed human beings who all too easily become self-focused and sinful. When we realize we've been absorbed in our own needs and desires, we can take the guilt we experience and go boldly to God's throne of grace (Hebrews 4:16).

Author and professor of spirituality Albert Haase discusses directionless guilt and graced guilt in *Coming Home to Your True Self*. Directionless guilt, he says, is useless, often paralyzes us, and leads to nothing profitable. This is the kind of guilt I experienced that morning at the grocery store.

Graced guilt, on the other hand, refers to God's divine gift and loving provision of grace for our wrongs. [2] "For it is by grace you have been saved, through faith—and this is not from yourselves, it is the gift of God—not by works, so that no one can boast" (Ephesians 2:8-9).

Graced guilt provides us with an opportunity to gain a deeper understanding of ourselves and can put us on the path of becoming who God created us to be. Self-condemnation, on the other hand, usually keeps us stuck. We get trapped in the destructive cycle of discouragement, self-hatred, and even despair.

Macy, like me, was briefly caught in the negative cycle of directionless guilt. But she then wisely moved into graced guilt. What I especially appreciate about the way Macy handled herself is how she willingly exposed, rather than hid, her flaws. She didn't discount it and say, "Well, I'm not so bad. We all get lured away from what's most important." She didn't let it slide until there was a huge crisis. She used the experience as an opportunity to gain insight into who she was and to recognize humbly how easily she could get her focus off others and onto her own selfish desires. She confessed, accepted God's grace (graced guilt) and asked me to hold her accountable for seeing herself as the flawed human being she is.

In coaching, I find my clients want to gain an accurate assessment of themselves. They want to understand how they may unintentionally be sabotaging their relationships at home or at work. They don't want to be self-deceived, nor do they want to miss the grace of God. The problem is that often, unlike Macy, they haven't learned the skills needed to gain a more objective view of themselves. Because self-awareness is so essential in all our relationships, the rest of this chapter is devoted to discussing four strategies needed to move from the darkness of self-deception into the transformative light of self-awareness.

1. Cultivate Honesty and Vulnerability

If you took an honest assessment of yourself right now, would you see that you have a tendency to lean toward any of the traits the apostle Paul describes in 2 Timothy 3:1-5? Are you ever self-absorbed, greedy, prideful, unforgiving, self-promoting, cynical, ungrateful, impulsive, or lacking self-discipline? Most of us would honestly have to say we've shown those characteristics at one time or another. Hopefully we are aware enough to take the necessary steps to ask for God's grace, strength, and wisdom to prevent those traits from becoming habitual behaviors. I love Henri Nouwen's prayer in *A Cry for Mercy*:

> Look at me, see me in all my misery and inner confusion, and let me sense your presence in the midst of my turmoil. All I can do is show myself to you. Yet, I am afraid to do so. I am afraid that you will reject me. But I know—with the knowledge of faith—you desire to give me your love. The only thing you ask of me is not to hide from you, not to run away in despair, not to act as if you were a relentless despot. Take my tired body, my confused mind, and my restless soul into your arms, and give me rest, simple quiet rest. [3]

Being vulnerable does not only refer to being open and honest with God and yourself. It also means admitting when you're wrong or when you are feeling insecure or uncertain.

Pat Lencioni, founder of a management consulting firm, has written several bestselling business books. He writes, "When we can demonstrate vulnerability to the people we live and work with, we build stronger relationships, affirm our trust in them, and inspire them to become more vulnerable themselves." [4] He goes on to say that people almost always sense or know when we are uncertain or feeling insecure. But we usually try to pretend we are invincible and hide our weaknesses. When we do that, we will see our credibility erode. A better option is to earn people's trust by being real and vulnerable. Admitting mistakes increases people's confidence in us.

People relate to us and feel connected when we are upfront about what we are experiencing. I recently read about an international spy who for years successfully took on different personas. She said she was able to earn the trust of her enemies because she was always honest about her feelings. For example, if she was in a terrifying situation, she verbalized how frightened she felt. And because her enemies were already discerning that emotion, they incorrectly assumed she was honest about other parts of her life.

2. Examine Your Motives

By being honest, Macy was able to ask herself, "Why did I so quickly abandon what I thought was important to me? What deep need was motivating me to focus on the money?" She recognized one motivating factor was the fear that she would never get out of debt. She would wake up in the middle of the night haunted by "what ifs." What if she lost her business? What if she couldn't pay her bills?

She also realized that there was a deeper motivating issue: She was trying to avoid the pain and shame she experienced growing up. Her family had little money and her classmates often mocked her tattered hand-me-down clothes and the shack of a house she lived in. As an adult she sought the approval and acceptance of others as well as the prestige that came with a successful business, stylish clothing, and a lovely home.

No longer blinded to this deep need to appear successful and earn the praise and acceptance of others, Macy resolved to be more aware of this vulnerability. She knew being more God-focused and less self-focused would enable her to maintain awareness of this motive.

Similarly, when I examined my motives for defending myself that day at the grocery store, I realized I did not want this person to view me as self-absorbed and uncaring. I wanted her to view me in a more favorable light, and I wanted to avoid the discomfort that came with seeing my true self. It hurt my pride to see myself as someone who does not always consider the welfare of others.

Recognizing my tendency to be self-focused enables me to humbly see my desperate need for God's love, grace, and forgiveness. The question is, will I admit my deep dependence on Him or will I hold on to my pride? As Paul tells us in 1 Peter 5:5, "Clothe yourself with humility toward one another, because, 'God opposes the proud but shows favor to the humble.'" A humble attitude also enables me to uncover the many other ways I attempt to create a favorable image of myself.

3. Recognize How You Try to Make Yourself Look Better

Have you ever been cleaning your house before guests arrive and thrown junk in the back of a closet or stuffed assorted clutter into a cupboard? Your house appeared clean as long as your guests didn't look anywhere you didn't want them to look. Few of us would show our guests the dirtiest room in the house, the most crammed closet, or our most disorganized drawer. We close the doors and avoid those places.

We do the same thing with our behaviors. We tidy them up. We hide our imperfections in an attempt to maintain a good image. Making excuses, minimizing bad behaviors, shifting blame, overcompensating, and playing the victim are just a few of the ways we try to keep a good image.

Making Excuses

My friend Gayle shared how she came to realize her tendency to excuse her behavior. In college she shared a room with two other girls. During a heated debate, one of her roommates said, "You know you always make excuses for yourself."

"I do?" Gayle said, stopping to think if this was true.

That one comment really hit home, Gayle said. "Now, fifty years later, I still frequently analyze whether or not I'm making excuses for myself."

I know more than once in the past when I was late for an appointment, I tried to make myself look better by saying, "I hit every red light on my way to the restaurant" or "I had to follow a school bus and stop every few minutes for miles." Making an excuse was easier than admitting I left home too late.

My ninety-one-year-old aunt is always ready in plenty of time. It's embarrassing to admit how many different reasons I've given her over the years for being late to pick her up. The problem with giving her all these different reasons is when I really *am* held up, she will assume I'm just coming up with another excuse. Even when we are no longer blinded to our excuse-making habits, it can be difficult to break the habit and accept responsibility for our tardiness or other poor choices. While we are focused on coming up with excuses, the people closest to us are usually not deceived. They know the truth. We are only deceiving ourselves.

Minimizing Bad Behaviors

Rather than making excuses for your actions or choices, you may minimize the problem. One person in a leadership class I attended said, "My weaknesses aren't so glaringly bad. If they were, I'd be motivated to address them."

The problem with her logic is that when her weakness does become glaring, she will probably be facing a crisis or an extremely embarrassing situation, all of which could have been prevented if she had been willing to address the issue earlier.

Shifting the Blame

Another way we see ourselves in a more favorable light is to shift the blame onto someone else. We're like the kids on the playground when a teacher tries to break up a fight. As kids, we might have said, "Hey, it's not my fault. He said my brother was stupid."

As adults, we might think, "It wasn't my fault I got so angry. He shouldn't have said those mean things. I wouldn't have broken those dishes if he hadn't said that. He started it. What was I supposed to do? Sit there and take it?"

I find that shifting the blame is something we do quickly. Accepting responsibility for the choices we make usually takes a bit more time and effort.

Overcompensating

In an effort to hide our flaws, we exhaust ourselves trying to earn the approval of God or others by doing good deeds. Because I made some pretty poor choices years ago, when I first became a Christian I exhausted myself trying to please God and those around me. I still have moments when I try to hide my flaws by overcompensating and trying to be some super Christian. The problem is no matter how many good things I do, it's never good enough. No matter how well liked I might be, I know the truth. My real motivation comes out of a prideful heart and selfish ambition rather than a heart that wants to help others.

Maybe you overcompensate and create a more favorable perception of yourself by attempting to rescue others. You work hard to fill their every need or comfort every pain. Or perhaps you give generously but instead of doing it out of love or because of a direction from God, you want to *look* kind, generous, or compassionate. Or maybe you believe those good works will erase any mistakes you might have made in the past.

Unfortunately, no matter how well liked or respected we are, we know that underneath our shiny veneer our real motivation is pride.

One question we can ask ourselves is, "Am I helping others out of a great sense of need and direction from God or from a great sense of self?"

Playing the Victim

When we play the victim we heap abuse and insults on ourselves in an effort to make others pity us and say reassuring things to bolster our self-esteem. One tipoff that you are playing the victim is if you notice yourself speaking in unqualified, broad generalities. You might say something like this: "Well, it's *always* my fault. No one cares about me. I'm *always* the one that causes *all* the problems around here. I *never* do anything right."

Whether we are making excuses, minimizing our problems, shifting the blame, overcompensating, or playing the victim, we fail to see ourselves objectively. We continue to live in denial, holding on to the comfortable perceptions of ourselves and remaining blind to the negative impact we are having on others.

4. Take a Continual Reality Check

Growing in self-awareness is not a once and done deal. My friend, Sue, found doing a Daily Examen* extremely valuable. At night she looks back over her day to see where God is at work and to reflect on why she behaved the way she did. She wrote in an email, "It is like Jesus and I are both looking, but not in a condemning way. As I sit with Jesus it's easier to be honest and really see things in a different light. I've found it to be very insightful and transformative in changing my behaviors and patterns of thinking."

It's dangerous to go through life without self-examination and times of solitude. Whether you are reading Scripture or praying, God, through the Holy Spirit, can keep you grounded in the truth. While solitude is valuable, isolation from others is not. When you are isolated, it's impossible to gain an accurate view of yourself because you become nearsighted and preoccupied with yourself.

Gaining a sense of reality means having people in your life who are willing to be objective and reflect back to you who you are. Author and speaker Pam Farrel refers to these people as her "fine-tuning friends." She says, "God uses them to tune us up so our lives become a beautiful melody reflecting our Lord." [5]

What if there is something about you that everyone has noticed, but of which you are unaware? Maybe you tend to talk about yourself too much or you are too intense. Or perhaps others see you as controlling or unmotivated. Wouldn't you want to see what others see about you? Wouldn't you want to understand how you are unintentionally sabotaging your relationships?

Like using the blind-spot mirror every time you want to pass another car, a more accurate assessment of yourself will help you avoid

---

* The Daily Examen is an ancient practice in the Church that can help us see God's hand at work in our whole experience. It is a technique of prayerful reflection on the events of the day in order to detect God's presence and discern his direction for us.

sideswiping those who cross your path. You'll also discover you are more humble and accepting of the flawed people you live with or work with every day.

If you are ready to shatter any distorted self-perceptions and gain clarity about who you are, routinely remind yourself that growing in self-awareness means being willing to see *what is already there*.

STOP: **Proceed with Caution**

1. Would you say you are receptive or resistant to growing in self-awareness? If you are resistant, list the reasons why.

2. What do you do first when you catch a glimpse of a selfish motive and uncaring behavior? Do you get depressed, try to hide imperfections, make excuses, minimize your behavior, blame others, overcompensate for your flaws to earn the approval of God and others, or play the victim? Or do you accept the pain and consequences, confess your poor choices, and remember that your guilt can be graced by God?

3. If you took a personal inventory of yourself today or this week, would you say you tend to be self-focused or God focused?

2

I Fail to Pay Attention to My Limitations

There is something deeply spiritual about honoring the limitations of our existence as human beings.

RUTH HALEY BARTON

I ran out of gas for the second time in six months," my friend shared. "I thought I might be close to empty, but when I started sputtering up the hill I knew I was in trouble."

"Didn't your warning light come on to alert you that you were getting low?" I asked.

"Yes, but now that the car is older the warning light doesn't stay on. I was busy and just didn't pay enough attention to how little gas I had left."

Just like our gas tanks, which have a limited capacity and need to be refilled to keep running, we have a limited amount of resources. We too can hit empty and need to be refueled. Like my friend who was too busy to pay attention to what little reserves he had left until he couldn't drive any further, we often get wrapped up in work and various activities, ignoring our rapidly diminishing reserves. If we keep ignoring the warning signs, we become exhausted and stall or stop dead. We don't take the time to replenish what has been depleted and fail to notice how we're living beyond our limitations.

We have only so much time in a day and only so many financial, mental, physical, or emotional resources. We all have our limits. When we fail to pay attention to them rather than accepting and accommodating them, our relationships suffer. Sometimes the consequences of overextending ourselves and exhausting our reserves are minor, and sometimes the consequences lead to irreparable damage.

My mother recently moved to a personal care home, which left my brother and me with the emotionally difficult and time-consuming task of packing up the home she'd lived in for 55 years. We decided to store many of her belongings in her attic and rent the other three floors of her home.

Since my brother lives 500 miles away and flew in for a long weekend to help me pack and move my mother's belongings, we had lots to do in a short amount of time. The first day we worked only a few hours, but the second day we weren't as wise. Not only did we pack box after box, but we carried them up three flights of steps. We failed to take breaks and didn't stop for lunch until mid-afternoon. By that time I felt weak and my stomach was queasy. The next day, I was forced to rest in bed at regular intervals with ice packs on my neck and back. I was exhausted and snappish with anyone who crossed my path.

I knew better than to push myself. But I ignored my limitations instead of accepting the reality that I have them. One of the reasons I did so was pride—I didn't want to look like a wimp to my strong, athletic brother. Thankfully, in this case, the consequences of trying to prove I was tougher than I really was could be remedied with a few good nights of rest and lots of apologies to those I offended.

Lindsay, however, would tell you that her failure to live within her limits had more disastrous consequences. "I thought I could do it all. I really did. I wanted to give abused children a safe, secure home. But I failed to realize and pay attention to what the stress and pressure of seven adopted children was doing to my marriage until my husband walked out the door. I needlessly wounded many people. I denied how unmanageable my life had become until I couldn't pretend any longer."

Another woman, Lillian, also ignored her limits and consistently wore herself ragged until she faced a life-threatening illness. "I liked being the go-to person at work," she said. "I loved being there for my family and friends whenever they needed something. I'm still finding that hard to let go of because that is how I related to people—by doing things for them." Then with a sigh of resignation, she added, "Now that my body has gotten my attention, I can no longer ignore the reality that for years I consistently pushed myself to exhaustion."

As Lindsay and Lillian recognize, serving others is a joy. But unless we are balancing all the busyness with our need to rest, recharge, and refuel our limited resources, the negative effects of our overloaded lives will catch up with us.

You might be thinking, *Wait a minute...God can do the impossible, and aren't there times when we are called to push beyond what seems humanly possible? Can't He replenish our depleted resources?*

Absolutely. God can do the impossible. In faith He often calls us to step out and do something that only He can do. But are you deciding through prayer and wise counsel to take action, or are you caught up in something that looks good but isn't God's best for you? What is your motive? Is it obedience to God and done in the strength He gives, or are you trying to prove something? Quite often we are trying to do things that are flat-out unhealthy.

Recognize the Warning Signs

Just as it isn't wise to ignore or discount the importance of the warning light on your dashboard, don't ignore or discount any signals alerting you that you're close to hitting empty. For instance, can you identify with any of the following comments?

- On most days I can make it all work, but I'm stressed out and I'm definitely not enjoying my life.

- I'm always tired. In fact, I'm tired, tired, tired.

- I just want to run away for a day or a week.

- I'm usually cranky and irritable with my children. I can honestly say I'm angry or anxious most of the time.

- I desperately need a vacation—by myself. I don't want to have to take care of anyone or anything.

- At any given moment I'm usually right at the breaking point of losing it. I feel angry all the time. I've surprised myself several times by how vicious I have become. I'm afraid I'm going to say or do something that will hurt someone.

• I always try to cram one more thing into my schedule. I can often do it, but then I'm exhausted.

Do any of these statements sound familiar? The sooner you recognize you're about to run out of fuel, the more quickly and easily you can do something to correct the situation.

Too many women I know are not only trying to live beyond their limits but are beating themselves up for not doing more. They fail to notice how they have taken on more and more responsibilities while at the same time they wonder why they can't do it all. They don't realize how they've exhausted their reserves and are "dangerously depleted"[1] until they can't keep going.

As Emily, one of my coaching clients, said, "I missed things that should have concerned me, but as the hectic pace of my life speeded up, I was lulled into thinking this driven pace was normal. My perceptions were dulled to the point that I did not even notice how tightly packed my schedule had become. As a result, I remained trapped in a vicious cycle of busyness because I had no extra time to notice how chaotic my life was. It wasn't until my ten-year-old son was having all kinds of behavioral problems at school that I was forced to stop and pay attention. I guess in his own way, he was screaming for me to slow down. Looking back over several months, I now realize how much my ongoing exhaustion and moodiness affected him."

Having the ability to adapt to our changing circumstances can be a good thing. But as Emily discovered, when we no longer notice how little we have to give to those we love, we fall prey to the insidious effects of living beyond our limits. Somehow as we drain our resources, the negativity slowly, almost imperceptibly, creeps into our relationships. If we compare our relationships this week to last week, we probably don't see any obvious difference. If we compare this month to last month, we might perceive a bit of a change. When we compare this year to last year, however, we will probably see a dramatic difference. Looking back several months, Emily said, "All the signs were there with my son but I failed to pay attention to how little time I gave him. I rarely had time to cook a decent meal or to just sit, chat, and hear what was going on in his life."

As Richard Swenson, author of *Margin: Restoring Emotional, Physical, Financial and Time Reserves to Overloaded Lives,* writes, "Our relationships are being starved to death by velocity. No one has the time to listen, let alone love." [2]

In your own life, how will you recognize when *you* are breathlessly traveling too fast or getting too close to hitting empty? What are the signals *you* need to be alert to?

Part of knowing the answer to that question involves knowing yourself. We all react differently. If you aren't sure of your warning signs, try to become more aware of your reactions or the thoughts that flash in your mind and heart whenever you encounter something unexpected. For example, when you live beyond your limitations, do you find yourself easily hurt and offended? Do you become hypersensitive to what someone is saying or doing? Or perhaps you become angry and lash out.

When I get close to empty, I find it difficult if not impossible to slow down and rest. My mind races with all the things I have to do and my anxiety is off the charts. I go into overdrive trying to do more and more, faster and faster.

Although we are all different, here is a short list of signs people have shared with me as they answered the question, "I know I'm trying to run on empty when I..."

- drink too much coffee or eat too much sugar to get energy
- am easily hurt and offended
- look forward to going to the dentist so I can recline and rest
- become self-absorbed and callous to the needs of others
- am too fuzzy-brained to drive safely and take reckless chances
- blow issues out of proportion

- incessantly beat myself up
- become ill
- become extremely anxious
- am too tired to make good decisions
- think only of my problems and my little world
- am dissatisfied or impatient with everything and everyone
- strive to please people and am convinced that I need their approval

Accept Your Limits

Rather than becoming discouraged about the fact you can't do it all, accept your limitations. View them as God's way of guiding you to do specific things.

As author and spiritual director Ruth Haley Barton has written, "Something of the will of God is contained in the very limits that we often try to sidestep or ignore. Living within limits is not in any way an acquiescence that is despairing, passive or fatalistic. Rather it honors the deepest realities of the life God has given us." [3]

Don't get caught at an unsustainable pace. Don't wait until a crisis stops you. Whether you have a tendency to be angry and hostile or depressed and passive when you push the limits, realize being spent and exhausted does you and your relationships more harm than good. Following are seven questions you can ask yourself to guard against becoming dangerously depleted:

1. Is Your Current Pace Sustainable?

If Emily had taken the time to step back and ask if her current pace was sustainable, the answer would have been *no*. She would have realized there was no way she could continue her frenzied pace and remain sane. Yet she never slowed down long enough to even consider this question. As a result, she never noticed how little she had left at the end of the day. Her son paid the price.

Even in troubling times, when we are forced into an unsustainable lifestyle for a season, we still need to carve out time to rest and renew. In those difficult times, ask yourself, "What are the essential activities I must attend to? What projects, commitments, or activities can I cancel or postpone?"

Authors Jim Loehr and Tony Schwartz write, "Sadly, the need for recovery is often viewed as evidence of weakness rather than an integral aspect of sustained performance. The result is that we give almost no attention to renewing and expanding our energy reserves. To maintain a powerful pulse in our lives, we must learn how to rhythmically spend and renew energy." [4]

2. Are You Savoring the Moment?

When we rush from one task to the next, we miss the beautiful bluebird outside our window—those magical moments only available in the here and now.

Instead of mindlessly moving through the day, be more present. Take time to slow down, enjoy, and appreciate what's around you. Instead of anxiously worrying about the future, take a few seconds today and be thankful for what God has given you right now.

3. What Are You Saying Yes To?

We often say *yes* before considering what is best for us. Yes, the job may need to be done, but that doesn't mean *you* are the only one who can do it. Yes, the task may be perfect for your talents or look like the only way to climb the success ladder, but that doesn't mean *now* is the right time for you to do it.

As Oswald Chambers advises in *My Utmost for His Highest*, "We must recognize the difference between burdens that are right for us to bear and burdens that are wrong." [5] Remember, God may have several things in mind for you but you won't know what they are until you seek His guidance.

One woman who always said *yes* and often regretted it later said, "I've learned to automatically say, 'Let me think and pray about it.' That way I don't fall into the trap of weighing myself down with too many responsibilities. I ask God for his wisdom—Is this the best investment of my time, energy and resources?"

Could someone else do this task, project or job? If so, then instead of saying *yes*, think about delegating it or giving another person the opportunity. If saying no seems impossible, then reflect on why you are struggling. Are you tempted to say *yes* because your identity is wrapped up in doing? Do you want to please the person who asked you? While the task or project might be a good one, is it best for you at this time?

4. Are You Intentionally Building Margin?

Margin is the reserve of gas you still have left in your gas tank when the warning light comes on. Margin is what enables you to drive to the gas station before you run out of gas. When we build margins or empty spots into our calendars, we are less likely to get caught up in a frenetic lifestyle.

In our lives, according to Richard Swenson, "Margin is the gap between rest and exhaustion, the space between breathing freely and suffocating. Margin is the opposite of overload. Margin grants freedom and permits rest. It nourishes both relationship and service. Spiritually, it allows availability for the purposes of God." [6]

Just like you schedule appointments on your calendar, schedule time to rest and renew your expended resources. Schedule the time and space to catch your breath. You'll still have times when you are frazzled, overloaded, and exhausted, but you will also know that you have time planned ahead to replenish your resources.

If you are unable to stop or slow down, ask yourself why. What are you avoiding? What are you afraid to face? As one woman said, "I was so busy I didn't have time to breathe. When I finally did start to create time to be, my mind was still racing. I couldn't just sit and be still."

If you are like this woman, then start with 30 seconds or one minute and simply focus on your breathing. As foolish as it would be to try to run a marathon when you can't run a mile, you need to slowly build up your tolerance for just being still.

5. Are You Spending Time on Activities that Recharge You?

What gives you pleasure? What refreshes you? It wasn't until I had a recurrence of breast cancer that I actually gave myself permission to nurture myself by gardening, reading, or doing something I loved. Before cancer, I rarely did that. If I did something for myself, then I felt guilty, thinking I was lazy or selfish for wasting my time. I thought I needed to be accomplishing more. Once I had the courage (and for me it took courage) to regularly spend time doing something rejuvenating that brought joy, I realized what a positive difference it made—how much it filled my soon-to-be-empty reserves.

What about you? If you had a whole day to do something that was healthy and enjoyable, what would you do? Would you read, sleep, watch TV, visit a spa, chill out with friends, watch a movie, shop, learn something new, listen to music, entertain a few friends, travel to the beach, exercise, run, golf, ride a bike, or hike?

Create a list of healthy stress relievers. Then give yourself permission to regularly do something that recharges you. Instead of viewing yourself as self-indulgent, look at it as a way to refuel. Caring for yourself can also be caring for others. In their book *Wellbeing*, Tom Rath and Jim Harter write that not only does 20 minutes of exercise a day improve our physical wellbeing, but can it also can also "boost our mood for the next 12 hours."[7] When we are emotionally up, we are less likely to experience the anxiety, hostility, resentment, or depression that often accompanies overloaded lives.

6. Are You Cultivating the Inner Life?

When we are so busy that we neglect our relationship with God, we are flirting with danger. As my friend Linda said, "When we are too busy for God, we are too busy."

I find that I so easily slip into the comparing and competing mode. Unless I purposefully focus on God and His pace and purposes for my life, I only become more driven.

Chrissie Grace, in one of her blogs, discusses the struggle of being caught up with our busyness rather than resting and spending time with God:

Yesterday at my Beth Moore Bible study we talked about "The Captivity of Activity." She asked us to look into our hearts and ask ourselves what we are trying to prove and to whom. I realized that I stay very busy sometimes to keep up my house and my projects even when perhaps I should be taking a much-needed rest. Am I trying to impress people I don't even really know? Am I trying to be the best wife, the best mom, the best artist, the best housekeeper, the best fill-in-the-blank? At the expense of time that I could be spending with God, resting and enjoying things, or playing with my kids? What would be wrong with not doing anything one day?[8]

Even a few quiet minutes a day can refresh us. For example, during the last morning of a hectic trip to California, I thought I really didn't have time to pray and be with God. Before I left for the airport I needed to do my hair and makeup, pack, strip the bed, and clean the bathroom. Because I had a view of the Pacific Ocean in the distance, I decided to take a few moments to enjoy the beautiful view. When I first sat down and looked at the view out the window, it was 6:45 a.m. and the ocean was gray. Fifteen minutes later, the ocean had dramatically turned to a lovely blue. At that point I felt the Lord whispering, "Georgia, the water didn't change in fifteen minutes—the light made the difference. When you take the time with me, even fifteen minutes of my light will make a huge difference in your life."

7. Do You Need to Adjust Your Expectations?

Sometimes we need to adjust our expectations of what we realistically can accomplish. Many years ago I read an article by Dr. Joyce Brothers in which she suggested we set our priorities by determining the three most important things we need to do and arranging them in order. She said doing this is important because we are really only effective for *four hours* a day.

Since I read that article, I've been much more realistic about my expectations for completing any activity that requires intense focus. For example, since I'm a morning person, after breakfast and my devotions,

I try to write, which requires intense mental focus. Spending the rest of the day on less demanding tasks, such as laundry and emails, creates a more doable pace for me. As a result, I'm happier and so are those around me because I'm not pushing myself to do more and more. One bonus is that I seem to get more done more quickly when I order my day this way.

When asked for the best health advice anyone has ever given her, Elizabeth Gilbert, author of *Eat, Pray, Love,* said, "My friend Suzanne once told me...'Just because you can do *anything* does not mean you can do *everything.*' I think it's something every woman needs to hear. It's time to back off from the crazy-making expectation that we should be able to do 7,000 things at once. Back off. Drop most of it. Let it go. It's an inhuman pace at which most of us live, and it will make you sick—and make everyone around you sick, too."[9]

How easy it is to slip into that "inhuman pace." Even vacations can be exhausting if we expect too much of ourselves. My friend Deb and her daughter went to Chicago to visit her brother's family, whom they typically saw only once a year for about two or three hours. She and her daughter wanted to do it all during their long weekend—see all the city sights, spend time with the kids, visit with the adults, catch a couple museums, have some one-on-one mother-daughter time, shop in dozens of boutiques, eat at famous restaurants, go to the park with the kids, watch them ride their horses, help with all the meal preparations, and more.

"We did only about half the things on our list," Deb said, "but we both arrived home absolutely exhausted. We overestimated our energy levels and underestimated the emotional resources necessary when being surrounded by three children we loved and who wanted to be with us constantly."

Deb says in hindsight, "There was a pivotal moment in the trip when my brother asked us what kind of visit we wanted: a relaxed time or a chock-full one. I wish we had stopped long enough to think about it. We didn't even pause to consider. It's been a week since we got back and I'm still tired!"

Why is resting so hard for some of us? Why has a frenzied lifestyle become natural and taking time to refuel so foreign? For some of us it might be out of habit. Others may have become addicted to busyness. And perhaps there are those of us who don't trust God to carry us through each day. Whatever the reason, we can choose to live differently. Exhausting our resources by working harder, faster, and longer isn't the answer.

Be willing to find another pace and rhythm of living—one that is different from the frantic, breathless one whirling around us. Choose to pay attention and honor your limits, renewing your resources instead of trying to run on fumes. In so doing you will honor those you love. Give yourself permission to take a breather.

STOP: Proceed with Caution

1. What signs indicate you are trying to run on empty?

2. In what situations do you try to push the envelope beyond what is reasonable? How would you say you are doing at expending and renewing your resources?

3. List three activities that recharge you and bring you pleasure. Are you willing to schedule and spend time doing one of them in the next week or two? (*Note:* You may need to give up doing something else to make time for renewal. What might you need to give up?)

4. Examine your priorities. What are the essential activities you must attend to? What projects, commitments, or activities can you cancel or postpone? Create a "To Do" list along with a "Not to Do" list.

5. Reflect or journal your thoughts and feelings on the following invitation from Jesus: "Come to me, all of you who are weary and carry heavy burdens, and I will give you rest" (Matthew 11:28 NLT).

3

I Resist the Season of My Life

Are you receptive or resistant to the
current season of your life?

Ever wonder why cars have the warning "Objects in mirror are closer than they appear" *only* on the passenger-side-view mirror? The mirror on the passenger-side is convex while the mirror on the driver's side is flat. While both types of mirrors enable us to see objects outside our normal vision, the passenger-side mirror provides a wider view of what is around us. The problem is that this broader image produced by the convex mirror makes objects look smaller than they actually are. Generally, when we see a person of average height who looks tiny, we assume the person is far away from us. That perception, however, is not true in the case of the passenger-side mirror. Even though a person or a car may appear small and far away, it isn't!

All car manufacturers are required to alert us of this distortion by printing a warning on the passenger-side mirror. But far too many of us either fail to heed the warning when driving or are clueless as to what is being communicated. As a result we're much more likely to make incorrect assumptions, putting ourselves or others in danger.

In the same way, many of us have a distorted view when it comes to the seasons of our lives. We often don't recognize the different seasons we face or understand how to adapt and adjust to them. Sometimes we erroneously believe that whatever season we are in will last forever. For example, I often hear mothers express frustration with their young children, sighing and complaining that their exhaustion will never end. As one mother whose son is now in his twenties said, "My son was always spitting up and I was sure nothing would ever change except for the three outfits I had to put on him each day. I honestly thought I always would be taking a burp cloth everywhere until someone asked me if I thought I'd need it at my son's high school graduation."

In contrast to the parents of younger children, I often hear the parents of older children express the belief that their life is over…forever. "I feel like my life ended when my children left home," one mother shared. "I know that's not true but it seems like my life doesn't have purpose anymore."

As a result of our distorted perceptions, we get depressed and often experience an increasingly deep dissatisfaction, especially about our lives. Unrecognized, this third blind spot, resisting or misunderstanding life's seasons, creates an inner restlessness that leads to friction in our closest relationships.

Rosalie, now in her early eighties, has lived in a personal care facility for five years. But Rosalie has refused to accept her physical frailness. "I don't know why I have to be here. No one visits me anyhow," she complains to her adult children. "I'm perfectly capable of taking care of myself." She constantly battles with her children, refusing to recognize that she is not capable of living independently. She is not receptive to this new season of her life and the sense of powerlessness it brings. She is miserable and so is everyone around her.

In contrast, Sylvia, who is eighty years old and lives in the same assisted-living facility, has been able to accept with grace the current season of her life. As a result, her relationships are marked with love, care, and concern. She acknowledges every kind gesture her family shows by saying something like, "I just want you to know how much I appreciate you and all you have done for me."

Much of the tension in your closest relationships can be eliminated when you are open and receptive, rather than resistant, to the current season of your life. If we can understand the different seasons and recognize their benefits as well as their limitations, we are more likely to accept the season we are in.

Understand the Different Seasons

Just like the warning on the passenger-side-view mirror alerts us to the distortions of what we see, God reminds us in Scripture of the different seasons He has designed so that we do not hold onto any misperceptions.

> For everything there is a season,
>> a time for every activity under heaven.
>> A time to be born and a time to die.
>> A time to plant and a time to harvest.
>> A time to kill and a time to heal.
>> A time to tear down and a time to build up.
>> A time to cry and a time to laugh.
>> A time to grieve and a time to dance.
>> A time to scatter stones and a time to gather stones.
>> A time to embrace and a time to turn away.
>> A time to search and a time to quit searching.
>> A time to keep and a time to throw away.
>> A time to tear and a time to mend.
>> A time to be quiet and a time to speak.
>> A time to love and a time to hate.
>> A time for war and a time for peace
>>> (Ecclesiastes 3:1-8 TLB).

When my only child, Kyle, was about three years old we recognized he had severe developmental delays. It was "a time to search," and search we did as we tried to find the professional help he needed. He had numerous neurological, educational, and psychological evaluations. No one offered any real help. But I kept searching.

After a couple of years, a friend suggested that maybe it was time to quit searching. "My husband just asked me yesterday," she said, "when is Georgia going to slow down and enjoy these years with her son?"

I look back at that time with a deep sadness. I completely misunderstood the season I was in. There were so many opportunities to trust God and lean on him, but I relentlessly tried to do it all myself. What's especially interesting is that when I finally did quit searching and got in step with God, we found a devoted teacher who provided the help Kyle needed. She transformed his life.

In contrast to that experience, when I was given a two percent chance of being alive in ten years because of a recurrence of breast cancer, I spent far less time resisting this new season and more time living in it. There were several reasons I was able to do this. First, the health challenge was so huge and my resources so limited that in some ways it was easy to admit to God and myself, "I can't do this. It's too hard. I give up." Second, I didn't feel the need to look strong and tough. I humbly acknowledged my fear and sadness and frustration. I sought medical help for the cancer and counseling to support me emotionally, but I had already learned with Kyle's problems that the seasons were not mine to control. Whether it was time to die or time to heal, for me it was time to surrender. As a result, a peaceful acceptance permeated all my relationships.

Being open and receptive to the different seasons of life is a challenge for most of us. One doctor told me, "Ninety percent of my patients who need to go into assisted living fight it. Some never accept it." He then added, "But it happens to most of us if we live long enough."

There are certain seasons we especially try to avoid. As one woman in her seventies said, "I see my friends investing all kinds of time and money trying to hold on to the beauty they had in their thirties. Yes, the expensive surgeries and costly cosmetics can help. But it's futile for them to think they can resist all the changes. All they need to do is visit a nursing home and realize that the time of old age does come."

We may try to manipulate things, but only God "changes times and seasons" (Daniel 2:21). They are not ours to force or control. Despite our best efforts, the wisest among us recognize that the seasons will change—sometimes gradually and sometimes abruptly.

Identify Your Season's Benefits and Limitations

Having a basic knowledge of the various seasons and understanding that they are not ours to change is important. But we also need to be aware of the current season we're experiencing along with its benefits and limitations. Every gardener knows the futility of ignoring the seasons. If it's winter it's pointless to plant my tomatoes outside even on the gentlest of days. While I may dream of having an earlier crop, one obvious limitation of Pennsylvania's winters is the possibility of sudden bitterly cold nights. It's usually well into April or May before I can safely plant my seedlings outdoors.

One of the blessings of winter, however, is that it gives me a chance to rest and renew. After working in my garden during the spring, summer, and fall, I look forward to the dormancy of winter. It provides me with the opportunity to curl up in front of a fire and catch up on my reading.

Recognize the Season You Are In

The seasons, as God outlined in Ecclesiastes, do not correlate to any one age or stage in life. You could be in your teens, the spring of life, when your mother suddenly dies and you abruptly find it is a time to cry and a time to grieve.

One of my friends is in her seventies. Some might consider her to be in the winter of life, but she's vibrant and full of energy. Having sold her old home, she's busy building a new one while traveling extensively. For her it's a time to build anew.

Even when your spouse or close friend is the same age as you, you may not be experiencing the same seasons. One of you may be facing a downward transition with the loss of a well-paying job while the other just received a promotion. For one it's a time to tear down and a time to grieve. For the other, it's a time to celebrate. Unless you pay attention to this and are sensitive to the needs of the other person, you will create all kinds of tension in your relationship.

Jealousy of the season someone else is enjoying also creates relational difficulties. For example, I know of a young man who recently lost more than 100 pounds. He feels so much better physically, but he is sad that some of his former friends no longer want him around. They tell him he's a different person from the old friend they knew. He maintains that the only thing that has changed is his size and his new healthful diet and exercise. Those former friends undoubtedly are jealous. They wish they could lose weight and become as disciplined as he has. But instead of being inspired by his example, they have chosen to let jealousy break up their friendship. For this young man, it is a time to embrace his new self and lifestyle and a time to turn away from his old friends who are rejecting him.

While you are identifying your current season, remember that it's possible to experience two seasons at the same time. Stacy, a good friend of mine, recognized that she was in the midst of both a time to grieve and a time to dance. Stacy and her husband were grieving the dissolution of their daughter's marriage, the poor choices of her ex-husband, the foreclosure of the young couple's house, and the debilitating medical problems their daughter was having. Once a week, though, Stacy and her husband carved out time away from the grief by taking ballroom dancing lessons. Their time to dance became an oasis of mental relief and emotional freedom. They looked forward to every lesson and were reenergized after each session. This enabled them to work through their grief and support their daughter.

Focus on What's Ahead

Although some of the seasons can be more challenging than others, all seasons carry blessings. Even amid the most difficult seasons, we can experience God like we never did before. We have the opportunity to lean on Him and discover He can be trusted.

All seasons have a certain beauty if we allow God's peace to fill us. Our natural tendency, however, is to focus on the limitations and losses that come with a season. Recently I waited in a long line for airport security. I overheard two young women behind me bemoaning the fact that they were now seventeen. "We'll never be sixteen again," the one said as the other discouragingly nodded in agreement.

The next week I crossed paths at church with a young woman who had just turned thirty. "How was your birthday?" I asked.

"Oh, it was really a hard one for me," she said. "I'm starting to notice all kinds of wrinkles."

I felt like screaming and yelling, "Let me tell you about the advantages of being thirty. You will never have smoother skin. You will never have more beautiful hair. Please appreciate the beauty you have now." Instead I said, "I remember feeling that way in my twenties and now I wonder why I did not appreciate that time more."

One of my coaching clients recently said, "At sixty-two I thought my life was pretty much over. I assumed my productive years were behind me. But when you mentioned that the fifties through seventies can be some of our most fruitful years for the kingdom, my whole attitude changed." Researchers have found this to be a productive season for women in part because our children are grown and we are no longer preoccupied by our careers. Our priorities have shifted and we can become more focused on the needs of others.

When a coworker complained about turning sixty to my friend Lynne, she asked, "Are you out of your mind? You're just getting started! Since I've turned sixty," Lynne said, "I've traveled to Paris and Barcelona. My friends and I love to attend concerts and I continue to create plenty of fun memories with my grandkids."

In Psalm 92:12,14 we read, "The godly will flourish like palm trees and grow strong like the cedars of Lebanon…Even in old age they will still produce fruit; they will remain vital and green."

Accept Your Current Season

Cooperating with the present season of your life can mean a time of struggling as you work through your feelings of frustration, anger, or sadness. But gradually you want to reach the point where you can let go of your disappointments and resentments so that you can embrace where you are.

A time of dying can be an especially difficult season to accept. Author and spiritual director Albert Haase writes about how one terminally ill young woman handled it. While visiting her one day he asked, "Margo, do you find it hard to die?"

"Not really," she replied instantly. "The suffering of the past year has forced me to let go of so many things—my privacy, the ability to go to the bathroom alone, the ability to feed myself and change the television channel. It seems like every day I'm challenged to let go of something else. And so, I've gotten really good at letting go and surrendering to the present moment. I suspect when death comes, it's just going to be another moment to let go and surrender." [1]

Instead of the inner tension and discontentment that comes when we refuse to align with God and the season we are in, this young woman experienced the inner peace that comes when we truly let go.

Acknowledge That Loved Ones Struggle to Accept

Even when you come to a place of total acceptance, you may find those closest to you are unable to cope or unwilling to accept where you are. For instance, one father was furious with his terminally ill daughter because she no longer wanted to try every experimental treatment that might be available. "I've been a guinea pig for years," she told me. "I'm exhausted and I'm done fighting. I can accept the fact I'm dying. Why can't my father do the same?" I'm sorry to say that her father refused to accept her pending death. As a result the last months of her life were filled with bitter battles.

I shared this young girl's story with my friend Gayle, whose husband had been fighting cancer for several years. After his death she said, "Hearing that story helped me to let go and understand it was time to quit searching for another treatment. Chuck was able to enjoy the last few weeks of his life with his family instead of enduring more procedures and all their nasty side effects." This is just one more example of the peace, love, and beauty we can experience when we cooperate with the seasons.

Lynne had a similar situation with her husband. One day the radiologist said, "I'm sorry to say that your husband does not have much time left."

"So what are we going to do about it?" Lynne asked. "I am not ready to accept the fact that he's dying."

"Your husband has accepted it," his doctor said. "He doesn't want to go through any more tests and treatments. You need to take the *I* out of it or you'll make these last days more difficult for him."

"Well I'm not going to accept it," Lynne said, and walked away.

After a time of reflection, she realized the doctor was right. The last few days with her husband were spent having intimate conversations. Even now, many years later, she continues to treasure those last hours they lovingly shared.

Adapt as You Struggle to Let Go

Maybe right now you feel more like Lynne when the radiologist first talked with her. You're refusing to accept this season. You're not willing to adapt to the times. If so, here are a few strategies that can help:

1. Find someone who is handling the same season well.
2. Seek the support and encouragement of others.
3. Remember a time you resisted.

Find Someone Who Is Handling the Same Season Well

Recently I attended a graduation party of my friend's son. I was delighted when my friend said, "This is not only my son's graduation party but my coming out party." Unlike some mothers who dread the empty nest, she was busy planning all the activities she could now enjoy because she would have the extra time and energy to do so.

Sometimes handling a season well includes preparing for the next. Not all of my baby boomer friends are focused solely on gathering and building up. Some are facing the time to tear down. In the last several months, Gayle has purged her home of everything she accumulated over the years. She has sold her home and she moved into a retirement community. "I've watched too many people become exhausted and overwhelmed with the job of cleaning out their parents' home. I decided I'm not doing that to my children."

Having recently packed up and cleaned out my mother's home, I too feel strongly that I don't want my son to face the same daunting task. For me, Gayle is a great example of handling the time to tear down well.

Seek the Support and Encouragement of Others

Depending on your season, you need to make new friends who understand where you are. Various studies have shown that the larger our social network, the better we journey through life's transitions.

Gretchen lost both her parents in two months. She joined a grief support group and met people who helped her adapt to this time of grief. Whether you choose to invest in a class, a coach, or a counselor, be willing to find those who can help you gain the confidence and skills you need while avoiding the pitfalls that can come with each season. If money is an issue, ask God to bring helpful people into your life. You will be surprised at the ways in which he will meet your needs as you remain open to tidbits of help from even the most unlikely sources.

I find people often need support and encouragement during the time of waiting. Simply reminding someone that not all seasons are fruitful is helpful. One of my coaching clients is in a time of waiting. Recently I reminded her that whether I'm talking about peach trees or cherry trees or the peonies in my garden, each one of them only produces fruit or flowers one season a year. Yet we often expect so much more of ourselves. We think that we should somehow be continually reaping a harvest.

Remember a Time You Resisted

Think about a time in the past when you refused to accept the season you were in. What regrets do you now have about that time? Now think about a season you adapted to and how God used that time to transform you.

Although I know the value of aligning myself with God and the time I'm in, I still find myself complaining instead of cooperating. Right now I'm in the season of caring for my eighty-eight-year-old mother and ninety-two-year-old aunt. In the last two weeks alone, my aunt has fallen twice. The last time she fell, she had removed her life alert button as she was changing her clothes. When she fell, she could not reach the button and lay on the floor for hours until a neighbor heard her cries for help. The neighbor called the police, who then had to break into her home. By the time I arrived, flashing lights and people filled the area. There were police cars, an ambulance, a fire truck, and neighbors everywhere. Although she was weak and terribly shaken, she was okay. The following emotionally draining days were filled with doctor visits, securing the services of visiting nurses, and filling out forms for her move to assisted living.

Days later I received a call from my mother's assisted-living facility. The nurse said, "I just want you to know that we called an ambulance and they are transporting your mother to the hospital." Once at the hospital I was informed that my mother's blood pressure was 203/111, she had a temperature of 104, and she could not form a complete sentence.

The next four days were a blur but slowly her health began to improve. The next call I got came from the social worker at the hospital. "Your mother is too weak to return to personal care, and the skilled nursing care in that same facility is filled right now. They have no beds available."

The next day or so I was consumed with finding another suitable facility, filling out more paperwork, and moving her clothes and belongings to the new location.

During that time I can promise you that the last thing I wanted to do was cooperate with the season. I wanted it over and behind me. At one point, when a friend prayed I would experience God's peace in the midst of these trials, I thought, *I don't need peace as much as I need these problems to disappear.*

Any little problem, like the service that transported mom to the nursing home and left her shoes back at the hospital, infuriated me. With God's help, I was able to be polite to people most of the time. But to those closest to me, I was not very pleasant to be around. Finally, after two nights of rest, I could appreciate the irony of writing about being receptive to the current season while being blatantly resistant to mine.

For me it was one more reminder that I don't get to choose the season, but I do get to choose how I respond. Will I continue to resent this season and complain to everyone who crosses my path? Will these maddening experiences harden my heart or soften it? Will I trust God and allow him to use this time to shape me into the person he wants me to be? Or will I waste my time and energy trying to avoid it?

Especially helpful during this time were a few words from Oswald Chambers: "You must allow *Him* to have His way with you, staying in perfect oneness with Him." [2]

Some seasons are exciting and others exhausting. Some seasons are short and some are long. Some are filled with wonder and some with disappointment. But one thing is predictable: They are ever-changing. And to grow more Christlike we need to be open and receptive to allowing God "to have His way."

Ask yourself these questions:

- Will I resist or surrender to this unfolding season?
- Will my relationships be marked with peace and love or with tension and turmoil?
- Am I living in the present season without ignoring or preparing for more to come?

One friend said, "I want to live in the present season but also prepare for the next. I realize what I do in this season will affect the next season. If I refuse to take care of my health, then most likely I will have health issues in the next."

I find it's the wisest men and women who are attentive to the times, willing to adapt and understand that seasons change. As a result, they not only live in harmony with the seasons but also with the people in their lives.

STOP: Proceed with Caution

1. What is your current season of life? How receptive or resistant are you to this time?
2. What are the benefits and limitations of this time?
3. Do you find that you are often trying to turn back the clock?
4. What seasons are those closest to you experiencing?
5. What are some ways you can encourage or support them during this season?

4

I Discount the Cost of Negative Relationships

The righteous choose their friends carefully.

PROVERBS 12:26

For several years whenever I stopped at the stop sign near my home, my view down the road was blocked by the spreading branches of a long row of spireas along the border of a cemetery. I could see only a short distance. The bushes had been neglected, and the intersection had become hazardous.

After several people complained of near accidents, the cemetery association pruned the bushes. The visibility was better, but then the shrubs grew back. People kept complaining, so the spireas were removed. The cemetery association then planted a row of knock-out roses at a safe distance from the road and has continued to keep them neatly pruned. The red roses are delightful, and now when I stop at that sign I have a clear view of the road in both directions and more peace of mind.

Like those uncontrolled spireas, we may all have some relationships that through the years have become a threat to our well-being. Most likely, things deteriorated slowly. We discounted the aggressive or destructive creep until one day, we discovered we had an out-of-control problem. If we reflect on the situation, we will probably notice that we failed to prune the relationship or maintain appropriate boundaries. Now that relationship may have a negative impact on our well-being and may need to be radically pruned or removed altogether.

More than twenty years ago, when treatments for a recurrence of breast cancer left me extremely fragile, I became painfully aware how subtly toxic some people can be. One day a friend took me to a chemotherapy treatment. For the entire 50-minute drive to my doctor's office, she recited one painful story after another about people who had faced cancer. After one particularly sad story about a five-year-old boy with cancer who died, I asked, "Can we talk about something besides cancer?"

She did. For five minutes. And then the litany began again.

After my treatment I was sick for two days. Previously, with that particular dosage of chemotherapy, I had never gotten sick. I thought it was more than coincidence.

It turns out that Jill Bolte Taylor, a neuroscientist, also had a similar experience in her thirties when a blood vessel exploded in her left brain and she experienced a stroke. "Once hospitalized, Dr. Jill could no longer walk, talk, understand language, read or write, however, accessing her right brain she was able to feel immense feelings of satisfaction and wellbeing. She experienced people as 'concentrated packages of energy.' Although she could not cognitively understand the doctors and visitors as they came in and out she could 'sense' what others felt. By closely studying their body language she would notice how some people would 'bring her energy' and others would 'take it away.'"[1]

I became convinced of how we bring or take away energy when on another occasion a different friend came to visit me. She shared how her husband, a doctor, had told her, "Georgia might look good now, but wait another five years and then see what she looks like. Who knows, she might not even live until Christmas."

At a time when I was trying to survive, her comment quickly eroded my hope and zapped my strength. For almost a week, I spent what precious energy I had talking to close encouraging friends and a counselor, trying to put the unsympathetic remarks in their proper perspective. I have no idea why she felt the need to pass on her husband's verdict, but I've learned the hard way that I needed to protect myself as much as possible from contact with such negative people. I had to distance myself from them and acquire the ability to say no when they wanted to visit or help me.

This was difficult for me because I had been taught to be kind to everyone. I had never recognized the need to set clear boundaries with some people. I had never realized that just like the weeds in a garden rob the flowers of vital moisture, nutrients, and sunlight, so too certain people in my life were robbing me of the vital energy I needed to fight cancer and heal. I could not afford to allow interactions with negative people to steal the few resources I had left.

In this chapter we are focusing on a particular type of relationship—friendship. We all have family, coworkers, or other acquaintances that we can't pick or choose. These people are just part of our lives, and we have to learn how to deal with them. And while we do choose our spouses and it's great if they are our best friends, the emphasis here is not on negative spouses. In this chapter, I'm talking about the relationships we choose outside of marriage—the people we allow to become our closest friends.

It's not wise to allow hurtful or hostile people into our innermost circle of friends. Yet far too many of us do this and even feel guilty when we consider distancing ourselves from these types of people. Leslie Vernick, counselor and author of *Emotionally Destructive Relationships,* said, "I'm dumb-founded by the number of women who have negative people and toxic people as a key part of their life. I think we are scared to see the truth about our relationships." [2]

Don't Be Blinded to the Price of Negative Friendships

You cannot afford to be blinded to the cost of negativity. You don't need to be fighting for your life to understand the high price you pay when you allow unhealthy or destructive relationships to be a consistent part of your life.

Current research validates the wisdom of Proverbs: "The words of the wicked kill; the speech of the upright saves" (Proverbs 12:6 MSG). Daniel Goleman explains in his book *Social Intelligence* that studies confirm "nourishing relationships have a beneficial impact on our health, while toxic ones can act like slow poison in our bodies." [3] He writes that like cold germs or flu viruses, "emotions are contagious." [4] When we are continually being exposed to negative, angry, hurtful people, the detrimental impact on our immune system is significant. Feelings "like disgust, contempt, and explosive anger are the emotional equivalent of second-hand smoke that quietly damages the lungs of others who breathe it in." [5]

Be willing to reassess your current friendships. Take a step back and ask yourself which of your relationships are life-giving and which ones are draining the life from you.

Friendships That Drain You

If you grew up in or currently live in an abusive environment, you may fail to notice the harmful effects of toxic relationships because these are the only kind you know. You may have never experienced a healthy relationship.

In her book on destructive relationships, Leslie Vernick says that a destructive relationship is not always identified by a single episode of sinful behavior but rather "pervasive and repetitive patterns of actions and attitudes that result in tearing someone down or inhibiting a person's growth. A destructive relationship is not the same thing as a difficult one. Learning calculus is difficult, but it leads to growth and to greater intellectual or mathematical maturity. On the other hand, ingesting cyanide is destructive. It harms and often leads to death." [6]

As a result of growing up with an emotionally abusive father, I was oblivious to the need to protect myself from more emotional abuse. Thankfully, many loving friends through the years have helped me to see my faulty way of looking at and tolerating damaging relationships. These friends also showed me what nurturing friendships really looked like—that there can be healthy give and take without the pattern of destructiveness.

At first, it isn't always apparent whether someone is a friend or foe, but with prayer and time it becomes clear. To help assess the possible negative impact of a friendship, here are four questions to ask yourself:

1. Does this person have a pattern of being negative, critical, and caustic? The friend who told me of her husband's dire prognosis had a history of making critical and depressing comments. Her words weren't

a one-time stick-her-foot-in-her-mouth remark. I, unfortunately, had failed to recognize the pattern. As you think about the people in your life, don't focus on just one conversation or one blow-up. Reflect on all the interactions you can remember and force yourself to think about the good and the bad.

2. Does this person tend to disappear when you are facing challenging situations? One friend disappeared during the time I was extremely ill with cancer. I don't know if my illness reminded her of the fragileness of life, if she found my illness inconvenient or unpleasant, or if there was some other reason for her absence. But during those tough times, she never called or came to visit. Once when I telephoned her, she was distant and aloof. As first century Roman writer Publilius Syrus said, "Prosperity makes friends; adversity tries them." Think about your hard times. Which of your friends have been there for you? Which of your friends have conveniently disappeared and perhaps reappeared when your life was going well?

3. Does this person violate the person God created you to be? God has given you strengths and gifts. It is one thing for someone to fail to affirm your gifts, but it is another if they mock or discount the very person God created you to be. If they don't understand you or accept you, if they insist you conform to a different image, do you really want this person to be in your innermost circle of friends? You can accept them just the way they are without allowing them to destroy who you are.

Haley is a girly girl and a people person. She loves pink, never has enough purses or shoes, always wears makeup, and dresses with a fun, trendy flair. She has great people skills and an athletic bent. She thought she was in love with a take-charge, protective guy. She thought he enjoyed her trendy flair and her gift with people. Over the months they dated, he often told her she was too friendly to others—girls and guys. He began to laugh at her trendy outfits. Then he began to tell her to stop working out or swimming, something she loved and needed as a stress reliever. After six months, her health began to deteriorate and she developed a number of aches and pains and injuries. Even her boss complained that she was not the happy people-person she once was.

Haley realized she had allowed her boyfriend to turn her into a different person. It took lots of courage and determination, but she ended the relationship and is back to being her healthy, outgoing self.

4. Does this person subtly erode your self-confidence? The negative effects of some friendships can be insidious. Do you ever walk away from a conversation feeling confused and discouraged and wondering what just happened? Or maybe you wonder if you are being too sensitive? You may have a sense that something isn't right but you can't put your finger on it.

Taylor said, "One friend at first appeared to celebrate my successes but there was always this destructive undertone to our relationships. Our families celebrated holidays together, but if my husband and I mentioned we were going to Florida in January, suddenly they were thinking of going to the Caribbean. If she noticed I bought a new purse, the next time I saw her she had a more expensive bag. In the beginning, I couldn't define what was going on, but I did notice how wearing the relationship was. I didn't say anything to her because ignoring it was easier than dealing with it. Finally, it got to the point that she was negatively impacting every area of my life and I could no longer ignore her toxic effect. I had to do something."

Like Haley or Taylor, you may determine a friendship is consistently detrimental to your well-being. What can you do? Does the relationship always need to end? What steps can you take to build a healthy buffer between the two of you?

Options for Draining Relationships

You don't need to end every negative relationship. As I said before, it is almost impossible to cut all ties to some negative people, such as relatives, coworkers, or ex-spouses. You can confront the person or create distance between that person and yourself. As a last resort, you may want to let go of the relationship.

Confront Them

One option is to confront the person. Before doing this, first seek God's wisdom and the advice of wise friends or a counselor.

Confrontation is usually not the best option with angry or unstable people.

Taylor prayed about her competitive, jealous friend. On the advice of a counselor, Taylor took the risk. During lunch with this person, Taylor said, "Please understand I am not in this friendship to compete with you. I would love to be friends and mutually support each other, but this competition is wearing me down. I am willing to give our relationship another chance, but you need to understand this isn't the type of friendship I want."

Taylor's friend quickly agreed that the competitive attitude wasn't helpful, but unfortunately her pattern of behavior continued. Several months later Taylor decided it would be best to limit her interaction with this person.

Distance Yourself

When possible, minimize your interactions with negative or toxic people. By creating physical distance between the two of you, you can limit some of the damage they cause.

You can be respectful to someone without inviting or allowing this person into your inner circle of friends. You can give love without allowing others to repeatedly rob you of vital energy and resources. And you can be forgiving without having an intimate connection— especially when you are vulnerable and weak.

When it's not possible to physically distance yourself, try to create emotional distance. Author and pastor John Ortberg suggests that even with good friends we should create a God space, "a kind of spiritual space between ourselves and the souls around us. That space is where God flows between you and me." [7]

Here's an illustration. One afternoon I sat on a garden bench watching the goldfish in my pond. One particular goldfish started nipping at the tails of the other fish. Some of the fish reacted by nipping back. I watched as they all swam around in a circle biting each other's tails. Finally, one of them broke away from the circle and swam to another area of my small backyard pond. The rest followed, creating a safe distance between themselves and the fish who liked to bite. Although they were all still swimming in the same pond, they were no longer being bitten because they were in another area apart from the instigator. Like those goldfish, sometimes we simply need to swim away.

Let Go of the Relationship

There are times when a friendship cannot be repaired. Perhaps trust has been broken and the efforts to patch things up have not gone well. With open hands, we need to let go and surrender those relationships to God. We need to grieve what we wish could have been, and the death of the hopes and dreams we had for those relationships.

Be prepared, however, for the other person to fight against such a separation or to not accept a new way of relating. When Kennedy worked up the courage to end a difficult friendship she said, "The next time we crossed paths the person began hurling negative comments at me. She said I was the most selfish person she knows and I need to know how much I hurt her. When I asked her if she really believed that I don't think of anyone else besides myself, she said, 'Yes.' I said, 'I'm sorry to hear that' and walked away. My parents and friends all told me I needed to end that relationship," Kennedy said, "but it was still extremely hard to do."

Like Kennedy discovered, getting rid of a toxic friend can feel overwhelming, and may require a sustained effort, like when I dug a new flower bed next to a field of weeds. That first year I was weighed down by the buckets of weeds that I had to remove in order for the flowers to grow. But each year the job became easier, because as I removed the weeds, I also eliminated the seeds they would have produced.

It's the same as we minimize or let go of the negative friendships. At first it's tough but with time it becomes easier. When we don't do the hard work of weeding, then our negative relationships become more deeply rooted, making them even more difficult to remove.

Recognize Some Friendships Are Seasonal

Some relationships, like some ministries, last only for a certain season. One woman emailed me and said, "It's hard for me to realize some friendships are seasonal because I don't want to be the kind of person who doesn't value friendships."

When Kimberly married at the age of twenty-four, she didn't have as much time for her friends. "I realized that one person, who had been a friend for ten years, was what I would call a 'pity friend.' She was more of a personal ministry for me and it came to the point that I did not have any extra time. I had invested what I could in her life and she had made the choice to remain emotionally crippled."

You can value people and the close connections you once had while also understanding that some friendships are only a significant part of your life for a limited time. Just because you no longer see or talk to that person doesn't mean you are throwing the friendship away because things have changed. Such pruning is good. We all have limited time and energy, and so we can only maintain a limited number of close friends.

During the years my son swam for a college team, another swim mom and I spent hours and hours sitting on the bleachers and watching our sons compete in swim meets. We traveled together to many of their away meets and shared the struggles of raising our sons. After our sons graduated from college, our paths no longer crossed. At first, we met for lunch and we telephoned each other. Over time, however, our chats became less frequent until they stopped. I haven't seen this friend for at least five years, although we exchange Christmas cards. We both have lots of fun memories of our times together and no ill feelings toward one another. Our lives have simply gone in different directions. While we no longer have the intimate connection we once had, I still treasure her being part of my life for that season.

Recognize Your Life-Giving Friendships

It is important to identify and minimize the negative relationships in your life so you'll have more time and energy to invest in the positive ones. Friendships are fragile and need to be nurtured. Even the best of friends won't always be affirming of you. They may disagree with you and tell you what you don't want to hear. "As iron sharpens iron, so a friend sharpens a friend" (Proverbs 27:17 NLT).

Overall, however, life-giving friendships energize us physically, emotionally, and spiritually. Good friends are accepting, encouraging, forgiving, and willing to listen.

Ways to Tend Your Life-Giving Relationships

The very traits that we desire in our closest relationships are the traits we need to extend to our friends. You tend to attract people like yourself, so be the kind of friend you want to have. You can nurture and deepen your closest friendships in the following three ways:

Be Accepting

"Accept one another, then, just as Christ accepted you, in order to bring praise to God" (Romans 15:7).

Understand the risk someone takes when they reveal a part of themselves they don't normally show or want others to see. Instead of automatically judging them, be someone who is worthy of their trust. Think about how you would feel if you were the person who was sharing a secret or a difficulty.

Grace, who had been married but now is single, said, "I dated someone I really was attracted to and struggled to remain sexually pure. I confided this to a friend and asked if she would pray for me. I will never forget the disgusted look on her face as she proceeded to give me a mini-sermon on purity. I felt lower than a worm crawling in the garden. Knowing she judged me rather than accepted me changed our relationship forever. After that, I never shared anything significant with her."

In contrast, when Grace asked a different friend for prayer and to keep her accountable, the reaction was the opposite. "She was so accepting and loving. She told me it's not a sin to be tempted as Jesus was also tempted in the desert. She committed to pray for me. What is most amazing, my desire for sexual intimacy dramatically lessened. I could not believe the difference her prayers made. I was so glad I had shared that with her. Having a friend who gets you and accepts you is wonderful, but I had to be authentic and real to experience that level of acceptance."

Be Encouraging

Weigh your words carefully with your friends. Consider whether what you are about to say will be affirming or discouraging to that person. While negative people's words stab our souls, we can use our words to lift the spirits of others.

Your friends will face challenging issues at one time or another. Whether they get sick, lose a job, go through a divorce, or experience the death of someone they love, they will need your encouragement. During her separation and divorce, Emily said, "I wasn't helpless, but I certainly felt that way. On more than one day I wasn't even motivated to get out of bed, but the love and encouragement of my closest friends made all the difference. I remember one day I received a beautiful card from one of them. She wrote, 'You are special to me and I know one day those gorgeous blue eyes of yours will sparkle again. Please know your beautiful qualities have added so much to me as a person.'"

Be Willing to Listen

Giving someone your undivided attention, with no distractions, is truly a gift. It is a powerful experience to hear the emotions underneath their words without feeling the need to fix them.

"When my brother was killed," Riley said, "I must have told my best friend how it happened over and over again. She never cut me short or suggested that she had already heard the story many times."

Sometimes friends are sensitive to what we're not saying. At one point my friend's son was stationed in a dangerous area in Iraq. The news reported that things were going badly in that area and since my friend, Linda, hadn't heard a word from her son in more than two months her fears and tears were close to the surface.

Although Linda was worried she did not say a word to any of the faculty serving with her during a week-long seminar because "I really didn't want to talk about it in the staff meetings or in a larger group because I knew I'd cry and I really needed to focus on taking care of the faculty and attendees."

Linda only interacted with people as needed and her friend Betty noticed. During a break when it was just the two of them, Betty asked, "Linda, is there anything bothering you?"

Linda told me, "Betty is a solid friend and I feel safe with her. She's also a solid Christian and she's a rock due to her relationship with Jesus, the Rock. So when she asked the question, I told her about my fears for my son. She prayed with me for my son. Her prayers comforted, encouraged, and strengthened me.

"The day after I returned home from the seminar," Linda said, "I had an e-mail from my son letting me know he and his soldiers were all okay. I immediately let Betty know how God answered our prayers!"

As wonderful as friendship can be, we need to realize, as Henri Nouwen wrote, "Friends cannot replace God. They have limitations and weaknesses like we have. Their love is never faultless, never complete. But in their limitations they can be signposts on our journey towards the unlimited and unconditional love of God. Let's enjoy the friends whom God has sent on our way." [8]

Choose your friends carefully. How far into your inner circle do you want to allow someone? How much of your time and resources is wise to invest? Every relationship has a cost, and with some the price is simply too high. Your life will never be free of difficult people, but you can make the choice to keep them out of your inner circle of friends. Even if you are deeply hurt by a friendship, instead of isolating yourself, surround yourself with the love and support of other, better friends. We are wounded in relationships, but we are also healed in loving relationships.

Robert Putnam is famous for having detailed the importance of good relationships. In *Bowling Alone*, he writes, "Countless studies document the link between society and psyche: people who have close friends and confidants, friendly neighbors, and supportive co-workers are less likely to experience sadness, loneliness, low self-esteem, and problems with eating and sleeping...The single most common finding from a half century's research on the correlates of life satisfaction, not only in the United States but around the world, is that happiness is best predicted by the breadth and depth of one's social connections." [9]

We often encourage our single friends when dating to be clear on what their deal-breakers and deal-makers are. We suggest they define the type of person they will *not* date. For example, some deal-breakers could be that they will not date someone who is controlling and manipulative, self-absorbed, or irresponsible. A deal-maker could be that they want someone who is committed to Christ, has a heart to serve others, and seeks to grow spiritually.

Whether we are single or married, what we often don't consider is that we also need to have clarity on what we will and won't settle for in our closest friendships. Maybe for you it's important for your closest friends to share your values and have a sense of adventure. For someone else, humor and trustworthiness are key.

Eliminate the Negative, Accentuate the Positive

Although I had never been warned as a child about energy-draining friends, what I discovered during those days when I was fighting for my life was that I needed to eliminate the negative as much as possible and then accentuate the positive. Like the flowers in my garden turn toward the sun, I decided to focus on the loving, beautiful connections in my life. I chose to appreciate and treasure the friends who cared for me. I know I would not be here today without all the support I received. The positive, nurturing, heart-to-heart connections counteracted all those sterile needles and machines I had to face and continue to warm my heart even on the chilliest of winter days.

I like to think that, like the flowers growing in my garden, my chosen friendships will continue to grow and thrive. But I know the only way they will have room to flourish is for me to pay attention and keep pruning and removing what doesn't belong.

STOP: Proceed with Caution

1. Proverbs 12:26 says, "The righteous choose their friends carefully." How intentional are you about choosing your friends?

2. Is there anyone in your life right now who you need to respectfully distance yourself from emotionally or physically? What friendships are you allowing to repeatedly rob you of time and energy? What can you do to minimize your interactions?

3. Which one of your life-giving friends needs your attention? What is one simple thing you can do to show that person your love?

4. Is God asking you to look at any negative or destructive behavior you have toward a friend?

5

I Justify My Poor Choices

To err is human, to rationalize even more so.

David Callahan

We were one hour into a five-hour road trip when I mentioned to my friend who was driving that I was having problems enjoying the ride because of the speed he was traveling. Even though he was going 25 miles per hour faster than the speed limit and his brother had just warned him to watch his "lead foot," my friend said, "Everyone else is speeding. Besides, if I stay within the speed limit, my slow driving could cause an accident."

Twenty-eight-year-old Noelle told her girlfriend, "I know the guy I spent the weekend with is disrespectful of women and has none of the traits I want in a lifelong partner. I know he doesn't share my faith. But I was lonely."

While shopping, Mia found a pair of shoes she loved but she had already spent more than she could afford. After purchasing the new shoes, she said, "I know they're too expensive and my husband will be furious, but I've been looking for shoes like these for two years. And they're so comfortable."

Natalie also loves to shop. She thrives on buying gifts for people and enjoys watching their faces light up when they open her presents. The problem is Natalie already owes several close friends hundreds of dollars. One of them asked Natalie, "Why are you spending money you don't have? You can't be doing that. You're already in debt."

Natalie quickly dismissed the question by saying, "God wants us to be generous with others."

Like the people in these true stories, we all have the amazing ability to come up with self-serving reasons for the poor choices and the compromises we make. This tendency to justify our actions widens, rather than narrows, any rifts already present in our relationships—just ask Mia's angry husband or Natalie's resentful friends.

To overcome this relational mistake, justifying your poor choices, it's important to do the following:

- Understand your tendency to justify a mistake.
- Avoid staying stuck in self-justification.
- Admit when you've made a mistake.
- Correct the mistake and stop repeating it.

Understand Your Tendency to Justify a Mistake

Although there are many reasons why we rationalize our actions and decisions, two of the most common ones are the desire to protect our self-image and the need to ease the inner turmoil we feel when our actions conflict with our beliefs and values.

Protect Your Self-Image

It's upsetting when we are faced with evidence that we are being jealous, uncaring, and even vindictive. Most of us want to see ourselves as competent, intelligent, kind, and honest. When Samantha made a careless error at work that cost her company thousands of dollars, she said, "I was mortified knowing I looked like an idiot to my coworkers. I couldn't sleep for days. I kept telling myself it was no wonder I did what I did. I'm overworked and underappreciated at my job. But with the help of my counselor I've learned to accept that I'm a fallible person who made a mistake...a mistake that hurt others."

Unlike Samantha, who was willing to see herself as less than perfect and as responsible for a serious error, Ben, a teacher, continues to hold tightly to the image that he is a good person. He's able to sleep at night, even if it's on his parent's sofa. A man in his forties, Ben recently had an affair with one of his former students and left his wife and two children, ages four and six. He told a colleague, "This Christmas was rough on the kids, but, hey, I wasn't out in a bar looking for a relationship. It just happened."

Foster Inner Peace

When we do something we know does not align with God's will and what we believe to be right, we experience an unsettling discomfort or even deep anguish. Our behavior and beliefs collide, and we begin to rationalize our actions in an effort to ease what is psychologically referred to as "cognitive dissonance." This is the inner turmoil we experience when our opinions or beliefs are incompatible with our behaviors. Say, for example, a man believes cheating on his wife is wrong, but he meets someone he is deeply attracted to and divorces his wife to marry this woman. He settles the cognitive dissonance he experiences by telling himself that since he met his soul mate his actions were justified.

When our actions conflict with our values or the attitudes we hold, we use justification or rationalization to alleviate our inner tension and the disturbing feelings that enter our consciences. In Ben's case, he remained trapped in self-deception because he told himself and others that the choices he made were acceptable since he wasn't looking for an affair. He happened to run into the woman at a local coffee shop. If God didn't want them to get together, Ben said, He wouldn't have allowed their paths to cross.

Another example of cognitive dissonance would be my lead-footed friend who believes that breaking the law is not wise and has obvious consequences and yet rationalized his speeding by saying, "I'm just going with the flow of traffic and to slow down might cause an accident."

Avoid Staying Stuck in Self-Justification

We must learn the skills needed to avoid and escape from the trap of self-deception. Here are four strategies that can help you to see what you currently are not seeing.

Take Time to Cultivate Self-Awareness

As historian and author Thomas Carlyle said, "The greatest of faults…is to be conscious of none."

Are you allowing time in your busy schedule to reflect on your day, your actions, your choices, and your attitudes? Take time to examine yourself and ask God to shine His light on you so that you see what is hidden in your heart and mind. Be open to seeing your less-than-glowing behaviors. "If we claim we have no sin, we are only fooling ourselves and not living in the truth" (1 John 1:8 NLT).

Be more mindful of your thinking. You may wonder how people like Ben can look at themselves in the mirror. Unless we pay attention to how we justify our actions, however, we also will remain blind to it. As one coaching client said, "Now that I'm looking for the different ways I rationalize my choices, I see how quickly and easily I do it. I try to catch myself when I begin to feel that inner pang of cognitive dissonance. I don't want to delude myself."

When we aren't open to seeing how we can distort reality, one justification will lead to another and another. For example, one night during a business trip, Janice accidentally landed on an adult entertainment channel. Even though she had heard of the addictive effects of porn, she decided to watch it for a few minutes. After all, what harm could it do? She was a smart person who was happily married and loved her husband. A few minutes led to a couple of hours. One encounter led to more. A habit formed but, Janice said, "I believed I could stop at any time. Who was I hurting anyway?"

Two years later Janice left her husband for someone she met on the Internet. "If you would have asked me that first night if I would leave my husband, I would have said, 'No way!'" Janice said with regret. "That one small compromise led to more compromises until I found myself far from where I thought I would ever be."

Acknowledge Inner Tension

When you feel upset, disturbed, or annoyed about something you said or did, pay attention. Assess what's going on. Is your behavior in conflict with your values, attitudes, or beliefs? For example, maybe you believe pleasing God is more important that pleasing people, but you're wearing yourself out trying to make others happy. You have little or no time to devote to what God has called you to do.

Instead of immediately seeking to ease your unpleasant feelings by justifying your choices, stop and live with the tension long enough to coach yourself through it. How would you complete the following?

I believe_____. And yet I_____. I justify it by telling myself_____.

I believe it is more important to please God. *And yet I* focus on being accepted, popular, and making others happy. *I justify it by telling myself* I have a servant's heart.

Here's another example: *I believe* two different people will have conflicting opinions and disagreements at times. *And yet I'm* always stuffing my opinions and feelings down so as not to create conflicts. *I justify it by telling myself* it's important to keep the peace.

Use Empathy to See Both Sides of the Issue

Empathy is not only understanding what someone is dealing with but also experiencing what they are feeling.

Tim Sanders, author of *The Likeability Factor,* says, "Empathy is different from sympathy. If you are sympathetic to others, your heart goes out to them and you feel compassion, but these are *your* feelings…If you are empathetic to others, however, you are not merely feeling sorry for them but are projecting yourself into their hearts as though you are sensing what it's like to be in their shoes…Sympathy is a sweet emotion, but it's not a connecting one. It doesn't give you the awareness of the other person that creates a bond." [1]

Staying stuck in self-justification might be sympathizing with a friend and saying, "I was only thinking of my friend when I told her I was staying home Friday night instead of going to the party. I didn't want her to know I was going somewhere without her. Anyway, she gets upset when I party too hard."

Empathy helps you avoid the trap of rationalization by seeing the same event from your friend's viewpoint. Ask yourself how you would feel if someone did to you what you did to them. Empathy enables you to realize your friend will probably be *more* hurt when she finds out you lied to her. She will feel as though you don't value her enough to be honest with her. With social media and mutual friends, the chances of her finding out the truth and being wounded are fairly high.

Be Curious Rather than Defensive

In addition to identifying when and how you justify your poor choices, be willing to ask yourself some of the following questions. You may need the help and feedback of a few safe, trustworthy friends. As bestselling author Dr. John Townsend suggests, be "curious rather than defensive." [2]

- Do I just want to be right?
- Could I have made a mistake?
- Is my identity wrapped up in looking smart, competent, and resourceful?
- Am I willing to accept the fact that I made an error?
- Am I willing to see the truth even if it means being wrong?
- Am I protecting myself from seeing who I really am?
- What am I saying to rationalize my behaviors?
- Am I empathetic to how others are impacted by my actions?

Until we are willing to entertain the idea we were wrong, we'll fail to see our blind spots and how skillfully we can distort reality. Failing to see our errors, we won't develop the humility needed to say, "I'm sorry."

Admit When You've Made a Mistake

Authors Carol Tavris and Elliot Aronson write in their book *Mistakes Were Made*, "To err is human, but humans then have a choice between covering up or fessing up." [3]

The TV show *Scandal* is based on the life of Judy Smith, who is president of a crisis management and public relations firm. Her list of clients include White House intern Monica Lewinsky, Chief Justice

Clarence Thomas, and quarterback Michael Vick. In an interview on *The Today Show*, Judy Smith said she advises people, "Admit it. Don't lie." She said that sometimes the cover-up is worse than the crime. [4]

Be Willing to Say You Were Wrong

Pat and her daughter bought two prom dresses and decided they would make the final decision at home. Her daughter had paid for both dresses, but would return with the receipt and the unworn dress on her day off. Later that night, however, Pat accidentally threw out the receipt. Pat realized her mistake a few days later and texted her daughter at work: "My fault. I can't retrieve receipt. I'm sorry and I will make it right."

Rather than creating an argument or insisting on being right for even minor mistakes, we need to use words like Pat did: "I was wrong. I made a mistake." While those words can be extremely difficult to say, especially for those of us who like to be in control, they mean a great deal to the people or person we have offended, hurt, or harmed.

More than one study has shown that when a doctor admits he or she made a mistake and apologizes and offers compensation to the patient or the family, they are less likely to file a malpractice claim. [5] This is especially true when responsible parties make changes to reduce the likelihood the mistake will be repeated. "Being assured that it won't happen again is very important to patients," says Lucian Leape, a physician and professor of health policy at the Harvard School of Public Health. "It gives meaning to patients' suffering." [6]

Be Willing to Accept Responsibility

Jennifer remained in an abusive marriage for years. She said, "I saw what I wanted to see. I thought I could fix him and if I just said the right thing at the right time he would change. I loved my husband and worked hard not to upset him. That meant ignoring a lot of the things he said and did. I justified my actions by believing if God wanted me to stand up for myself, He would give me the words."

Not only did Jennifer fail to stand up for the respect she deserved, but she failed to intervene on her daughter's behalf. Now free of the abusive marriage, Jennifer sees how she never challenged her husband on his abusive treatment of their only child. "My daughter carried a lot of anger and resented that I just allowed her father to hurt her. She was right," Jennifer said. "I have to accept responsibility that I hurt her by hardly ever saying anything."

Whether it's a minor incident like being late for a dinner party or a major offense such as failing to protect your daughter from an abusive spouse or partner, rationalizations such as, "we are just fashionably late" or, "I know she's hurting but she has to look at the big picture" don't cut it. Like Jennifer, we need to apologize, accept responsibility, and, where possible, correct the mistake rather than repeating it.

Correct the Mistake and Stop Repeating It

Since one justification leads to more justifications, we want to resolve our mistakes and repair our relationships as soon as possible. To do so, we need to expose rather than hide our errors and take the necessary steps to prevent justifying the same poor choices in the future.

Count the Cost of Doing Nothing

A number of years ago, I spoke at a conference with several other speakers. Before the event, all of the speakers were given free professional makeup touch-ups and hair styling at a nearby home. The hair stylist put a hot curling iron on a cherry table and forgot about it. By the time she realized her mistake, the table had a deep mar on the finish. Since it wasn't her home or table, she felt horrible. She told the event coordinator about the accident but failed to mention it to the homeowner. Later, when I asked the event coordinator about the homeowner's reaction to her burned table, the coordinator said, "I didn't say anything to her. The stylist was going to take care of that."

I have no idea how long it was before the homeowner discovered her damaged table. Whether it was days or weeks, I'm sure she was as upset about not being told as she was disappointed to find her table damaged.

Yes, it is painful to say you are sorry and ask what can you do to rectify the mistake, but think how the other person feels if you do nothing. In the case of the burned table, talking honestly with the owner shortly after it happened would have been a far better choice. We believe people will think less of us when we do something wrong. In actuality, when we have the courage to admit a mistake and offer to correct the damage, people usually respect our courage, honesty, and willingness to do what is right. They may even think more highly of us than they did before we committed the error. When we cover up, lie, or justify ourselves, what we ultimately damage most is the relationship.

Once when I was discussing how we justify our mistakes and attempt to shift the blame instead of owning and correcting them, one college freshmen said, "That's what everyone my age does. Instead of taking responsibility, they say, 'It wasn't my fault.' Besides, who wants to admit you did something wrong? I've gotten into more trouble than I would have if I said nothing."

She's right. Admitting to the police that you ran that red light definitely increases the odds you will get a ticket, but the bottom line in our relationships is that right is still right. As a friend said to me, "Georgia, I've learned that the right thing to do may be the hard thing to do, but relationally it's always the right thing."

Listen to Those Who Can Be Objective

Be open to listening to the advice and suggestions from the truth-tellers in your life. Although it might be hard to hear, the "wounds from a friend can be trusted" (Proverbs 27:6).

Lisa was in love with Brandon, a great-looking, successful salesman. She was determined they would get married. Although her friends could see Brandon's positive assets, they were deeply concerned about his negative qualities. He was self-centered, deceitful, and controlling. They hesitated, however, to share their opinions because from past experience they knew Lisa rarely listened.

One day as Lisa was talking about Brandon, her friend said, "Tell me what you especially like about him." After Lisa shared the different things she adored about Brandon, her friend asked, "Is there anything that concerns you about him?"

Lisa touched on each one of her friend's concerns. She talked about how he never asked how she was doing and that when she was sick he disappeared for several days. She mentioned that several times she had discovered he had lied about being home when he was really with another woman at a restaurant.

When Lisa's friend said, "Those are valid concerns. Are you sure you really want to marry him?" Lisa quickly changed the subject.

The longer Lisa holds tightly to the idea she will marry Brandon, the harder it will be to admit it is not a wise choice. The more she pours into their relationship, the more difficult it will be for her to change her mind.

Lisa could save herself much heartache if she would be open to listening to her friends' comments and suggestions. She could ask herself, "What are they seeing that I'm discounting? Why is it so difficult for me to hear what they are saying? Am I just holding onto the dream of being married rather than looking at Brandon's real character?"

We are all guilty of making a decision and then stubbornly holding onto our point of view despite overwhelming evidence that we are wrong. We distort reality, and, instead of seeing our blind spot, we continue seeing what we want to see. To correct our errors rather than repeating them, we must also be willing to surrender our need to be right.

Let Go of the Need to Be Right

The desire to be right is especially frequent in our closest relationships, with marriage often being the biggest battlefield. When we feel we have been heard by our spouse or friend or coworker, it is easier to let go of the need to be right. But how do we let go when someone isn't willing to hear how you feel wronged?

First, ask yourself these questions: *Am I looking at this situation or at the other person with a magnifying glass while viewing myself and my actions through rose-colored glasses? Am I so focused on how that person wronged me that I've become blind to his or her good qualities?*

Second, letting go of your need to be right also includes forgiving the wrongs of others. Realize that sweet, kind, good people are just as likely to justify their poor choices as people who are mean and filled with hate. Once you understand it's natural to want to justify a poor choice, be gentle rather than judgmental of those in your life. After all, self-justification does have a protective quality to it.

Learn from Your Mistakes and Change

Judy Smith, the crisis management expert I talked about earlier, said, "In every crisis, there are opportunities. We all have issues and problems; it's how we navigate them and the lessons we learn from them that count."

Mistakes are part of life and, usually, are not fatal. Over the years I've been single, I've made many poor choices in dating. And I'll confess I usually did a great job of justifying my choices to myself and others by saying something like, "Well, at least I have someone to do things with." But as time has gone by, I also have to admit that I've learned many things. I've learned to become friends with a man before investing a great deal of time and energy in a romantic relationship. I've learned the importance of looking at someone's character instead of focusing on chemistry. I've learned to listen to the wisdom of my closest friends.

Couples who have married and successfully grown "together over the years have figured out a way to live with a minimum amount of self-justification."[7] They have learned the value of admitting when they are wrong. They have learned to be empathic toward each other and treasure each other's positive qualities. They realize they themselves are flawed, and if they aren't willing to take the time to examine their own hearts and minds they'll lose the ability to see their blind spots.

Self-deception is the worst kind of deception because we believe all the self-serving reasons or lies we tell ourselves rather than owning our poor choices and feeling remorseful. This very behavior causes people to distance themselves emotionally from us rather than want to be closer.

Admitting a mistake can be unpleasant, costly, and humbling. It's not something we like to do. But being open to seeing the blind spot of self-justification means we can be open to learning and making positive changes. How would Mia's marriage improve if she worked with her husband and learned to live within her means? He would probably feel she respected him more and appreciate her efforts to be financially responsible. What if Natalie, who loves to give gifts, could curb her spending until she has repaid her friends? Maybe instead of feeling manipulated and wanting to distance themselves from her, they could enjoy being with her.

What if, instead of fighting to be right or justifying your poor choices, you took a risk and apologized?

STOP: Proceed with Caution

1. How frequently do you try to protect the image of yourself as a caring, positive, and honest person?

2. How would you rate yourself on acknowledging and admitting you made a mistake?

3. How frequently do you focus on others' wrongs while justifying why you're right?

4. Are you willing to ask someone who is trustworthy and objective what self-defeating behaviors you tend to justify?

6

I Avoid the Pain of Reality

Will you avoid the pain and enable it to destroy you, or
will you face it and allow God to transform you?

When my son, Kyle, was in college, the girl he adored and had dated for months abruptly ended their relationship. As a typical mom I worried about him and called each day, asking, "How are you feeling? Are you eating? Are you hanging out with your friends?"

"I'm okay, Mom," he'd reassure me. "I just want to pretend it didn't happen."

Weeks later, I grew concerned that he had overloaded his social calendar to avoid his heartache. "I'm glad you are getting together with your friends," I said one day on the phone. "But please don't ignore your broken heart. If you do, it will never heal properly. And that will negatively impact all your future relationships. I know it's tough, but you have to press through the pain."

"Mom, don't you think I know that?" he said. Kyle is an all-American swimmer. "Every athlete knows that you'll never improve if you don't press through the pain," he continued. "It's the only way to get stronger and faster."

The same principle applies to our emotional and spiritual growth, which in turn impacts our relational health. It's all those unpleasant and difficult experiences that produce greater endurance, strength of character, and hope (Romans 5:3-4). But that only happens when we are willing to confront any anxiety-producing, discomforting, or difficult situations.

We so often fail to notice all the ways we try to escape from what is real. We don't realize how wishful thinking contaminates our relation-ships. For example, Tricia, whose out-of-control spending led to a sep-aration from her husband, has continued to accumulate an enormous amount of debt. "For years I turned a deaf ear to my husband," she said, "thinking he was a tight-wad. I always went ahead and bought all those cute little dresses because they looked great on me. But now that the bank has towed away my car I'm forced to see what I tried to ignore."

You might not be steering away from the pain of excessive debt like Tricia, but each one of us evades what is uncomfortable or unpleasant. As spiritual director Albert Haase writes, we believe "we must avoid pain, blame, criticism, disgrace and loss. And so we quickly develop skills that shun, shield, steer clear of and sidestep any form of emo-tional embarrassment or physical pain."[1]

Evading What Is Emotionally Painful

One single woman who ended her engagement after several years said, "Even though I knew we weren't the best for each other, I contin-ued to be with him because the thought of ending our relationship was just too depressing." She looked at me and asked, "Why did I ignore what I knew was true?"

Even *just thinking* about what we may lose or considering some-thing that's distressing can elicit tremendous fear and anxiety in us. Dr. Daniel Goleman says that if we even perceive something is going to be painful we have the amazing ability to deaden that pain by simply "tuning it out."[2]

Until we admit to ourselves that pleasure, comfort, and ease are our preferences, we will fail to see the thousands of different ways we numb, soothe, or slip away from any hurt or pain. We will continue to hold onto our self-created illusions of what is true until reality breaks through one way or another. When we hide the truth from ourselves and others, we hinder our growth and open ourselves up to all kinds of relational problems. As Dr. Goleman warns, "When this faculty for self-deception is mobilized to protect us from anxiety, the trou-ble begins; we fall prey to blind spots, remaining ignorant of zones of information we might be better off knowing, even if that knowledge brings some pain." [3]

Researchers who study consumers are well aware of our tendency to evade the painful. They know those who shop with cash will focus more on the cost of an item and purchase less than those who use credit cards. "There's an emotional pain associated with handing over hard currency that curbs spending," Gregory Karp said in the *Chicago Tribune*, "as opposed to mindless purchasing when forking over plastic." [4] When we pay with hard-earned money we immediately feel the pinch. Credit cards make spending money less real, and the less real it is the more we splurge.

Maybe you aren't shielding yourself from financial reality, but perhaps you're deadening your anxiety about the troublesome state of your marriage or avoiding that uncomfortable conversation with your coworker. Be alert and begin to pay attention to the different ways you try to steer clear of what is difficult.

Here are a few examples of ways we convince ourselves that bypassing what's emotionally uncomfortable or taking the path of least resistance is a good thing:

If I Start Crying I'll Never Stop

Cynthia, whom I met at a conference, shared how her sister had betrayed her. With a quivering lip and tears welling in her eyes she said, "I refuse to allow myself to cry about it. I'm afraid if I start to cry I will never stop."

I offered her a tissue. "Don't forget how healing those tears can be," I said. "At first it feels like they'll never stop, but gradually they will."

Denying how deeply crushed she is allows the emotional pressure to build. One day in the future Cynthia will probably find herself venting at an inappropriate time and place. Or she may be reduced in public to that puddle of tears she's been working hard to escape.

If I Face Reality the Pain Will Never Go Away

If your heart-wrenching pain comes from the loss of a child, spouse, or parent, you might never be totally free of *all* the pain. But the ache will eventually become less crippling as you confront what no longer can be, protest what has happened, and process your feelings.

If you fail to press through the pain, however, it will remain and create more pain. You'll never get to a place where you can begin again.

If I Face the Truth the Pain Will Destroy Me

One woman whose husband recently left her said, "I can barely breathe. Even if I do fall asleep, I wake up agonizing over every little thing. I'm not sure I can survive this. I have to do something to get rid of the pain before it kills me."

It's normal to want to numb your sorrow with something like food, medications, or busyness. It's normal to believe you don't have what it takes to handle the pain. It's normal to become paralyzed with fear. But when you evade those crippling feelings, you're also evading your need for God. "And now just as you trusted Christ to save you, trust him, too for each day's problems; live in vital union with him" (Colossians 2:6-7 TLB). Not only will you not be destroyed but you will develop even greater endurance. Scripture reminds us, "When all kinds of trials and temptations crowd into your lives my brothers, don't resent them as intruders, but welcome them as friends! Realize that they come to test your faith and to produce in you the quality of endurance" (James 1:2 PHILLIPS).

If I Face the Truth Everything Will Change

"You don't understand," Sonya said. "When I face the truth that my husband, who is addicted to drugs, is becoming more hurtful and abusive to me and my son, then everything in my life will have to change. We will have to move. I will have to find a job. And I'm not sure I will be able to provide for us."

I frequently have to remind women like Sonya that seeing what is true does not always mean you have to make dramatic changes overnight. In her case that would not be wise or safe for her or her son. While Sonya does need to be honest with herself about the unhealthy state of her marriage, she also needs to prayerfully seek God's guidance, obtain professional counseling, and secure legal advice. Then she will be better equipped to face the challenges and determine the best path for the two of them. To remain in a toxic situation for years and pretend all is well will only lead to bigger problems. As we are reminded in Scripture, "A prudent person foresees danger and takes precautions" (Proverbs 27:12 NLT).

Pain is the signal that something is wrong. If my knee is constantly throbbing and I ignore the pain, I can do further damage to it. Whether I see a doctor or give it a rest, I must give my knee the attention it needs if I want it to heal.

In the same way, be willing to take the necessary steps to protect yourself from further emotional injury. Maybe you have a friend who repeatedly hurts you. By admitting this relationship isn't a healthy one, you're more likely to take the steps needed to heal and to gain insight into what's really going on between you.

Sometimes confronting the truth about a relationship just means having that discussion you've been evading. Recently, a dear friend said some things that were hurtful to me. I knew she did not intentionally mean to cause me pain. At first I didn't want to admit to myself how much I hurt. "No big deal," I told myself. But the pain did not go away. It only got worse.

For me, to pretend nothing happened was like putting a little Band-Aid on a gaping wound. I prayed for God's timing. I knew I ran the risk of hurting our friendship if I responded poorly. Thankfully our discussion helped each of us to understand the other person's point of view, and we both benefitted. If I had denied my hurt feelings I would have missed the opportunity to build an even deeper relationship.

It isn't usually the pain of reality that destroys a realtionship as much as it is failing to deal with the truth. What's hurtful isn't always harmful.

Distinguishing Between Hurtful and Harmful

As author and licensed psychologist Dr. Henry Cloud says, "There is a big difference between 'hurt' and 'harm'…We all hurt sometimes, especially in facing hard truths, but the process helps us grow…That is not necessarily harmful. Harm is when someone is damaged. Facing reality is usually not a damaging experience, even though it can hurt." [5]

There are many situations where the harm comes when we run away from the truth. When I was first diagnosed with breast cancer, I rarely used the "C" word—cancer—except during doctor appointments. I kept my medical records in a file folder labeled *breast lump*.

I only told my family and closest friends that I had cancer and usually added with a whisper, "Please don't say anything to anyone." The less anyone talked about it, the easier it was to pretend it wasn't happening to me.

One day my brother was especially frustrated with my denial of the cancer diagnosis. He put his face in front of mine. "Georgia, look at me!" he said "You need to hear this. *You have cancer.* You don't have a breast lump. You have cancer!"

I knew he was right. I knew I had been desperately trying to hold onto my distorted view of what was happening.

Denial isn't all bad. It is a defense mechanism, which at first kept me from crumbling in a heap on the floor. Denial helped me to put one foot in front of the other. But if I was to make wise choices about my treatment and get well, I needed to face the fact that I did have cancer. Not to embrace that reality would be harmful.

Having surgery to remove the tumor did hurt, but ultimately that procedure and the other treatments were healing.

Gaining from the Pain

Instead of dodging what is painful, think about how your relationships might be different if you chose to confront rather than cushion yourself from uncomfortable situations. What would happen if instead of reacting to the difficulty you concentrated on the ways you can grow wiser? What if you believed that what hurts you will ultimately help you?

Check Your Perspective

More than once I've been locked into a hopeless view of a situation and had to ask myself, "Is there another way I can look at what's happening?" For instance, when I'm struggling over a writing project and pondering how to best communicate an idea, I quickly become frustrated and want to give up. Thoughts like *I'll never get this right* race through my mind. I often reach for something to eat to soothe my anxiety.

If, however, I remind myself that fresh new ideas usually emerge in the midst of these struggles, I'll be less apt to run from the pain and run to the food. I'll be more likely to press through the unpleasantness because, even though it's uncomfortable, I've learned this creative tension usually produces great ideas.

When things are unpleasant or distressing it helps to reevaluate the way I'm viewing my situation. Years ago I heard a sermon that included a story about a Chinese farmer. In the story, a poor Chinese farmer's only horse runs away. When his neighbor hears this troubling news he says to the farmer, "What bad news! I am so sorry."

The farmer only looks at his neighbor and says, "How do I know this is bad?"

A few days later the horse returns, bringing a wild stallion along. When the neighbor hears about this he says to the famer, "That's wonderful. What good news."

The famer looks at him and asks, "How do I know this is good?"

The farmer's only son tries to tame the wild horse and accidentally breaks his leg. Upon hearing of the accident, the neighbor says to the farmer, "What a tragedy this is."

To which the farmer only says, "How do I know this is bad?"

Shortly after that a war breaks out and the emperor requires all young and able-bodied men to fight, but the farmer's only son is spared.

This story and the question, "How do I know this is bad?" has resonated with Kyle and me over the years, especially when things looked bleak. One of these times was at the last NCAA swim championship of Kyle's college career.

Ever since high school, Kyle's dream had been to win an event at the national college swim championships. It was a feat that he never quite accomplished, so his last chance during his senior year was crucial. On the second day of this last NCAA swim meet, it became apparent that

Kyle was not "tapered." In swimming terms this means Kyle was not swimming at his maximum speed. He had not rested enough from his training during the season to allow his body to fully recover.

That night as we sat across from each other in the college gymnasium Kyle worked hard to hold back tears. Finally, he started to sob. Deep gulping sobs. "I just wanted to win one event, Mom. That's all I ever wanted." He gasped for air. "That was my dream. Now it will never happen!" He swiped at the tears running down his face with the sleeve of his warm-up jacket.

"Kyle, I am so sorry," I said, trying not to create a scene. "Believe me, I wish I could change things."

Neither one of us slept much that night. Everything in me wanted to protect Kyle from the harsh reality of his life.

The next morning I dragged myself back to the natatorium for the last tormenting day of finals. As I watched Kyle swim his laps in the warm-up pool, it hit me. *How do we know this is bad?* I quickly walked over to the balcony railing, leaned forward, and waved one arm to get Kyle's attention. When Kyle got out of the pool, I shouted, "How do we know this is bad?"

He looked at me questioningly.

"How do we know this is bad?" I slowly repeated as loud as I could.

His face lit up with a big smile.

I sighed, knowing my son was going to be okay. Perhaps this was the good that came out of the hurt: He was willing to entertain the idea that something positive could come out of a painful life lesson.

Like Kyle, be willing to temporarily distance yourself during those distressing and unpleasant moments and check your perspective. Ask yourself, "How do I know this is bad?"

Seek an Outside Perspective

When you get stuck on one way of looking at a situation, seek the viewpoint of a trusted friend. Find someone who can be objective and doesn't have a vested interest in whatever it is you're facing. You want someone who is not afraid to say what may be difficult to hear or what you are resisting. You may even want to temporarily stay away from those who tell you only what they know you want to hear.

Jennifer, a coaching client, said, "I don't have anyone in my life who will be really truthful with me. All my friends are afraid to tell me what they really see." If your friends are *afraid* to be truthful, maybe you need to reflect on how you've treated honest people in the past. Did you get angry? Did you get defensive? Did you really listen to what they were saying?

If you don't have any candid people in your life, intentionally try to cultivate that type of relationship with someone who is safe and worthy of your trust. When you are stuck in a hopeless view of your circumstances, you need someone to encourage you and remind you of the truth that your hope is ultimately in the Lord.

Once when I was facing lots of endings and many closed doors, a friend said, "I know you are facing lots of tough stuff, but don't lose hope. Even if you can't see it right now, God can bring something new and good out of this mess."

Her hope echoes Isaiah 43:19 NLT:

> For I am about to do something new.
>   See, I have already begun! Do you not see it?
> I will make a pathway through the wilderness.
>   I will create rivers in the dry wasteland.

Pay Attention to the Ways You Escape Reality

It's critical to identify how you evade or try to escape from what is real. What activities do you rely on to make yourself feel better? How do you make it easier to pretend things really aren't that bad?

When I asked a group of women how they tended to run away from the emotional pain or anxiety in their lives, they shared these things:

- spend hours on Facebook
- shop
- eat

- play computer games
- read novels
- get wrapped up in the lives of TV characters
- sleep
- text or talk on the phone
- watch movies
- socialize
- drink
- pour myself into Christian service

None of these actions are inherently evil. They become a problem, though, if they prevent you from seeing what is true in your life. For example, when you overeat to soothe your anxiety, you gain weight. When you notice the extra pounds, you become more frustrated and anxious. More concern about your weight usually means more eating. You're now trapped in a vicious cycle. Instead of escaping the original pain or problem, you've created more problems in your life.

Trish found herself using eating and shopping to shield herself from the frustrations and challenges in her marriage. In one of our coaching sessions she said, "I want to stop running away from what is real and true. I'm tired of shrinking back whenever anything gets difficult. As vulnerable as I feel right now looking at the mess my life has become, I know facing reality will ultimately make me a stronger and better person."

Make Time to Do Something You Enjoy

Facing the truth can be tough. We can only handle so much reality at a time, and usually do a better job of coping with it in small doses. Taking a break to catch your breath is not the same as escaping from the pain. Give yourself time to rest and renew your depleted resources. But do it knowing you will get back to facing those tougher issues.

We talked earlier about how Deb and her husband took dance lessons in the midst of their daughter's difficult divorce. What do you enjoy? What will refresh you or give you temporary relief? Whether you like to visit a garden, ride your motorcycle, listen to music, or paint, alternate these moments of distraction with the times when you tackle reality.

Take Action

Action is critical to prevent more pain. Take the blinders off and don't be afraid to see your world as it is, not as you wish it could be. Keep reminding yourself that as tough as it is to face reality, it will be even tougher and possibly more dangerous to deny or ignore it.

Earlier we talked about how one woman put off ending her engagement because the thought of it was too depressing. What I didn't mention is that before she mustered up enough courage to break off their engagement, she and her fiancé bought a home and lived together. Because she failed to take action earlier, she created more heartache and upheaval later.

Another single woman who continued to date someone she knew had a history of cheating said, "I just didn't want to be alone. I figured it was only a matter of time before he did the same thing to me." One year later, after she had become even more attached to their relationship, he left her for another woman. "Now I'm not only alone but tormented by the fact that I allowed it to happen. A lot of this heartache could have been prevented."

As Albert Haase writes, "Never flee from the present moment, even if it is painful, confusing, sorrowful, distressing or heartbreaking." [6]

It's humbling for me to realize how Christ never tried to circumvent suffering. He never shied away from what was unpleasant or distressing. Even when tortured, he did not look for a way out. He modeled this for his disciples and showed them and us how we can do the same.

> Then Jesus went to work on his disciples. "Anyone who intends to come with me has to let me lead. You're not in the driver's seat; *I* am. Don't run from suffering; embrace it. Follow me and I'll show you how" (Matthew 16:24-25 MSG).

At the start of this chapter I talked about how Kyle tried to numb the heartache of his break-up with a busy social life. His initial reaction was to deny how much it hurt and escape the emotional struggles that come with grief and loss.

Kyle had learned through swimming, however, that pressing through the pain, although challenging, is not to be feared. He knew all too well—no pain, no gain. Whether it was physical or emotional pain, he understood he would be stronger and better in the end.

Grieving was painful for him but not harmful. Kyle talked candidly to a close friend. He prayed and wrote about his feelings. The two of us prayed together. He even wrote a beautiful poem to help himself work through the heartache.

"Pain is purposeful when we respond to God with open and receptive hearts," writes pastor and author Jeff Manion. "We discover that the place we most want to escape has produced the fruit we most desperately crave." [7]

Put your hand in the hand of God and be willing to look at your situation truthfully. Trust Him to help you press through it. The problem might not disappear and you might daily cry out, "God, I can't handle this. It's too much." But eventually you'll discover God has taken the painful and the unpleasant and used them to transform you into someone better and stronger than you were before. I know…because it happened to me.

STOP: Proceed with Caution

1. Is there any truth you're refusing to look at right now because it is uncomfortable or because it will bring more pain and upheaval into your life?

2. What problems have you failed to see in the past? Be willing to seek the truth and pray for the Lord's revealing light.

3. How do you tend to numb the pain or run away from the tough stuff? (Shopping, busyness, watching TV, spending too much time on Facebook, etc.)

4. Are you willing to ask God to show you how to face the pain, especially when it's difficult?

7

I Minimize the Power of My Emotions

Emotions can help you and they can hurt you, but you have no say in the matter until you understand them.

TRAVIS BRADBERRY & JEAN GREAVES

E motions. We love them. We hate them. We ignore them. We stuff them down. We project them onto others. But whether you tend to bottle up your feelings or dump them on others, you have been blindsided by them at one time or another and probably hurt someone as a result.

Most of us underestimate the influence of our emotions and overestimate our ability to manage them. If you have ever experienced road rage, you know this to be true. This seventh relational mistake, minimizing the power of our emotions, influences every aspect of our relationships. The first step we can take to gain clarity about this blind spot is to recognize that "our brains are hard-wired to give emotions the upper hand."[1]

Emotions Have the Upper Hand

All sensory information (sights, sounds, smells, etc.) you experience first travels through the emotional part of your brain (amygdala) before it arrives in the rational part (frontal lobe). Although the rational part of the brain does influence our emotions and vice versa, the sensory data is first felt emotionally. As Christian life coach Lisa Gomez Osborn says, "Emotions are so much louder than anything else in your brain."

To understand how to best manage these loud emotions, you need to recognize that whenever you have an experience that elicits an intense emotional response, the emotional part of the brain, the amygdala, takes control. Daniel Goleman coined the term "amygdala hijack"[2] to describe the ability of the emotional part of the brain to take over our mental capacity during strong emotional reactions. The amygdala takes control by reducing the flow of blood and oxygen to the rational part of the brain and redirecting these resources to the emotional part.

For the health of your relationships, recognize that the amygdala has a tendency to overreact. Think intense rage. Crippling sadness. Self-loathing shame. If you ever wondered, "What was I thinking when I responded that way?" you probably experienced an amygdala hijacking.

During her college years Lydia was deeply hurt by her boyfriend's betrayal of a confidence. In the heat of the moment Lydia texted a scathing note: "You are pathetic. You obviously have a loose bolt or you wouldn't be so determined to destroy me. I hope you are miserable the rest of your life."

"Later, when reasoning kicked in," Lydia said, "I realized how over-the-top my text was. I can't believe how viciously I lashed out at him. I can't believe I said those things. That's not like me at all."

Three signs indicate you're experiencing a hijacking: an intense emotional reaction, a sudden behavioral response, and later, recognition that you responded inappropriately. Studies have shown that just being aware you're having an amygdala hijacking is enough to give you the ability to deal with it appropriately.

Scripture reminds us of the wisdom of slowing down before overreacting. James 1:19 says, "Everyone should be quick to listen, slow to speak and slow to become angry." Similarly, Proverbs 14:17 reminds us that "short-tempered people do foolish things" (NLT).

In the last chapter we discussed the importance of understanding the difference between what is hurtful and what is harmful to us. One of the reasons we can so easily confuse the two is that when we experience an emotional hijacking, the protective, over-the-top reaction of the amygdala leads us to assume a situation is harmful.

At a young age, Nancy witnessed her neighbors' barn burn to the ground. Now when she smells smoke, she instantly feels anxious and her body becomes tense. Seconds later, when her rational mind kicks in, she can more clearly determine if she is safe. Nancy has learned that taking a few deep breaths while she counts to ten gives her time for the blood and oxygen to return to the rational part of her brain. Then she can accurately assess her circumstances.

Understanding that your emotions have the upper hand is the first step to avoiding being blindsided by your feelings. The second step is to recognize how you can grow in emotional awareness.

Increase Your Emotional Awareness

Naming the feelings that are rumbling around inside of us is freeing. Too often, however, we don't have the ability or the desire to give a voice to what we're experiencing.

More than half of us struggle with verbalizing our emotions. In one large study testing more than half a million people, researchers found that only 36 percent of those tested were able to accurately identify their emotions. The other two thirds lacked the skill to identify and manage them.[3]

The good news is you can learn the skills to increase your emotional awareness. Here are some strategies to get you started:

Take Time to Name Your Emotions

Ask yourself, *What is it I'm feeling?*

After her husband of 47 years passed away, Gayle said that grieving was such uncharted territory for her that often she wasn't sure what she was experiencing. When she took time to ask herself *What do I feel?* she was able to identify and isolate her anger, loneliness, or sadness. Naming emotions might be like learning a new language. Remember that discounting or hiding your feelings means that you will continue to carry their emotional weight.

After I spoke about anger at an event, a young woman came up to me, sobbing. "I've been angry at God for eleven years but I've never told anyone. I did not want to admit it to myself or anyone else." Visibly shaking, she said, "My fiancé killed himself a few months before our wedding. I'm angry at him, at myself, and at God for allowing it to happen." As she gradually expressed her bottled-up feelings, I noticed a change in her whole appearance. Giving a voice to her anger enabled her to feel so much lighter and freer that she even looked different.

When I asked her why she'd suffered in silence for all those years, she said, "I thought I was the only person who felt this way. I wondered if there was something wrong with me. My family never talked about anger."

Don't Rush to Judge

How often do you tell yourself, *I shouldn't feel this way?* How frequently do you think, *I'm being so immature. Why am I so hurt by my friend's stupid comment? Is something the matter with me?* Rather than labeling your feelings as good or bad, accept them. After you have accepted them, you will be in a better position to understand what they are trying to tell you. By taking a moment to sit with Jesus and reflect about your feelings, you can better determine what is going on and how to express those emotions constructively.

For instance, as Wendi stood in the long line to pay for her groceries, she grew impatient. When the woman ahead of her emptied her full cart and pulled out a stack of coupons, Wendi sighed loudly. *Why did I have to be behind this lady in line?* Immediately she felt guilty. After all, she told herself, as a Christian she was supposed to show patience and self-control.

Rather than immediately judging herself as an example of a poor Christian, Wendi could use this situation as an opportunity to look at her resentfulness. Is she feeling resentful because she feels entitled to an uninterrupted schedule? Is she tired or hungry? Is she worried that she will be late for her meeting? When we quickly judge ourselves, we often miss the opportunity to more accurately assess what's really going on inside.

Recognize that Moods Change Like the Weather

In just one day, Tara rode an emotional roller coaster. Her car broke down, her boss gave her an unexpected raise, a client decided to go with another company, she got a text saying her sister-in-law delivered a healthy baby girl, and the garage called with an estimate of $800 for repairs.

While it's important to acknowledge and pay attention to your feelings, recognize how quickly your emotions change and how easily you can be blinded by them. Just because you feel something is true does not mean it *is* true. You might feel rich but that doesn't mean you have limitless cash to spend. You might be hurt or irritated that your friends seem to team up against you, but that doesn't necessarily mean you need to end your relationship with them.

Acknowledging that emotions can go up and then down within seconds helps you avoid making major decisions, like getting married, changing jobs, purchasing a new home, or terminating a relationship based *only* on feelings. The wisest choices are made by following the three *H*s: Listen to your Heart. Use your Head. But, most importantly, follow the leading of the Holy Spirit.

Journal About Your Feelings

Journaling has consistently been a great way to clarify what I'm feeling. Rather than stew over my irritability or frustration, I write about it. I have a whole shelf in my office with handwritten journals I've filled over the years. Writing in a blank book, however, is not the only way you can journal.

You may be like my friend Nancy who thought journaling was only about writing by hand. She has started but never finished several journals. When Nancy had to journal for a Bible-study class, she complained to her friend Sara who replied, "You're great at journaling. You email me your thoughts and feelings all the time." That was the revelation: Her fingers prefer typing. Now Nancy types her journal entries and keeps them in a computer file folder.

Ask Someone You Trust

You can become more emotionally aware by asking a few close trustworthy friends: "How do my emotions impact you? Have you ever been uncomfortable with my anger? Do I tend to be irritable or anxious?"

While asking this can make you feel uncomfortable and vulnerable, you will gain clarity on how you and your emotions are affecting your relationships. Natalie, who had been furious with her husband's spend-thrift ways, said, "I was blind to the fact that my resentment against my husband was leaking into all my relationships until a close friend mentioned the grudge I was carrying."

When Christine asked a dear friend how her emotions impacted their relationship, she said, "It was encouraging to hear how I often bring positive energy into our conversations."

Be aware. Do you tend to bring energy to others or deplete the emotional resources of those you interact with? What feelings are you carrying with you?

Also understand that others can help you become more emotionally aware even when you don't ask for direct help in identifying your feelings.

Tyler's parents passed away within weeks of each other. Going through their possessions and cleaning out their house was time-consuming and tedious, but also emotionally draining. He quickly recognized his need for help and called a good friend, Steve, who came over every night after work to help and give moral support. More objective than Tyler, Steve would say things like "Give yourself permission to be sad" or "Obviously that's connected to a fun memory."

One night Steve had another commitment, so Tyler asked someone else to come over. With a let's-get-down-to-business attitude, this person pushed Tyler to make quick decisions and totally disregarded the emotional connections he had to his parents' possessions. At that point, Tyler recognized how helpful Steve's emotional support had been. Steve helped to expose some of the unidentified feelings rumbling inside Tyler as he prepared to sell the home he grew up in.

Don't Automatically Believe What Others Say

When I was in fourth grade, my family moved in the middle of the school year from the suburbs to the country. We moved from a comfortable home I loved to a farmhouse I hated. It was a fixer-upper without an indoor bathroom. I missed my old friends and felt sad and angry. Instead of validating the loss I was experiencing, I was criticized: "Georgia, you shouldn't feel that way. You're only thinking about yourself. You'll be fine. You just need to make new friends."

I now understand my protests, caused by the pain of the move, were a normal response to loss. I was honestly expressing my displeasure. But the message I incorrectly internalized was that I was bad or wrong for even having those feelings. As a result, I became ashamed of my feelings. Then my unexpressed anger grew into resentment and bitterness I held onto for years.

If someone judges your feelings, don't immediately conclude that person is correct. For example, I often hear someone judging a friend for being stuck in grief. Maybe the grieving person is stuck but maybe her friend does not understand that she can only handle the pain of loss in small doses. Maybe her friend doesn't realize how long the grieving process can last.

Don't immediately discount your own feelings or allow others to judge them. In addition, be aware that sometimes people project their own feelings onto you. Emma's husband, for example, repeatedly accused her of having an affair. "I can't trust you," he said. "I know you are lying to me. You don't really love me."

Confused, Emma sought out the advice of a friend, saying, "I do love him. I don't understand why he's accusing me of something I am not doing."

Several months later, Emma accidentally discovered her husband was the one who was not being faithful. *He* was the one having an affair.

Manage Your Emotions Instead of Letting Them Manage You

Emotional Intelligence refers not only to your ability to identify and understand your feelings but also to your capacity to *manage* those emotions.

Instead of allowing your emotions to run rampant, make them a powerful ally. Take time for self-examination. Own your feelings and consistently deal them. Just like we routinely deal with our physical trash, carve out the time and space to regularly address your emotions. Here are a few ways you can turn those negative and potentially toxic feelings into something positive.

Know Your Triggers

We all have strong emotional reactions to certain attitudes, people, or situations. For Wendi, a long line in the grocery store is one of them. For Amy, it is her daughter. "I continue to be amazed how fast we can go from a casual conversation into a heated argument," Amy said. "She's now married and lives in another city, but we still can get into an intense debate pretty quickly, even over the phone. I've learned to take a deep breath and just listen instead of trying to fix her problems."

Knowing your triggers enables you to respond rather than react to people or situations you normally find irritating. If you can't avoid your triggers, you can plan how you will deal with them.

For one of my friends, Rachael, any visit with her parents can be an emotional trigger. Looking back twenty-plus years later, she knows her childhood was full of emotional abuse. If she needs to stop by their house, she is careful always to bring another adult with her. Through years of trial and errors, Rachael also has discovered that spending holidays with her parents is too stressful. Instead, she invites her parents to her house for a holiday meal and also invites a few guests who are not family members. As one counselor told Rachael, those guests "help your parents not to be themselves."

Listen to Your Body

Have you ever noticed that certain physical symptoms accompany particular emotions? As one woman told me, "When I'm anxious, my stomach churns. If I feel overwhelmed, I often get a headache. I just want to sleep when I'm depressed.

"But," she said, "when I realize these connections, I can take measures to help myself. I might drink a glass of milk for my upset stomach, take an aspirin for my headache, or go on a brisk walk to wake me up." Listening to your body can help you to more quickly and accurately identify a feeling, often before you are able to verbalize it.

Pay Attention to the Ripple Effect of Your Feelings

Just like a pebble thrown into the water creates ripples, our behaviors and reactions unintentionally influence those around us. Emotions are contagious. If everyone who crosses your path seems to be resentful, check yourself. You may be the one holding onto bitterness and it is influencing those around you. Or if you feel like everyone is being cranky and snappish, ask yourself if there is something eating away at you that you haven't owned. Is your irritability inadvertently affecting the mood of others?

In the same way, you sometimes can positively influence the mood of those around you. At lunch one day, Caren finished her dessert and sat back to observe the other women around the table. She later told me, "I realized how our pleasant lunch had soured into a gripe session aimed at our husbands. Since I had no interest in contributing to the complaints, I tried to change the mood. I said to my friend, 'You know one of the things I appreciate about my husband? He's incredible in bed.'"

The women stopped talking and they started to laugh.

"'So what's your husband good at?' I asked them. And I watched as the emotional tension evaporated. I heard things like, 'My husband is great with the kids.' 'My husband can fix anything.'"

Within minutes Caren had successfully been able to change the focus and mood of her lunch group.

If our days are marked by emotional outbursts or we're detached from our feelings, the ripple effect we have is one of hurting and wounding the people we love. Ask yourself, "Am I inspiring good feelings? Or do I unintentionally tend to bring negative ones into the conversation?" While we all have down days, we want to pay attention to moods around us on a typical day.

Recognize the power of your emotions, for good or for bad. Pay attention to your feelings. What are they telling you? Has someone deeply hurt you? Are you angry about something that just happened? Are you irritated and frustrated that nothing went as planned? As my friend Leslie Vernick says, "Our emotions are meant to inform us, not rule us." [4]

When it comes to harnessing your feelings for good, just remember this: The degree to which you are aware of and able to manage your emotions is the degree to which you will positively and powerfully make a difference in the lives of others.

STOP: **Proceed with Caution**

1. How emotionally aware are you? Would you say you tend to resist, discount, or detach from your feelings?

2. How well do you manage your emotions? In general, are your emotions your allies or your adversaries? Do you harness or neutralize potentially toxic emotions or do they control you? Do you tend to inspire good feelings or bring negativity into your interactions with others?

3. Dr. John Townsend suggests being vulnerable and asking those closest to us questions like these: "Did I hurt your feelings when I said that?" "On most days do I bring energy or deplete your resources?" "How are you and I doing?"

8

I Deny the Impact of the Past

We have to look back in order to move forward.

can still hear the deep bass voice of my driver's training instructor: "Georgia, a good driver is a defensive driver. You have a rearview mirror for a reason. Use it."

In addition to looking in the mirror, he also taught me the importance of responding to what I saw. "If someone is tailing you too closely," he said, "speed up a bit if you can do it safely. But always stay within the speed limit and be mindful of road conditions."

Most of the time when I'm driving, what's behind me isn't a threat. Occasionally, I notice a car bearing down on me or moving to pass me on the left before it disappears into my blind spot. I've learned that being aware of what's going on around me is key to safe driving. Being aware also helps me respond appropriately rather than overreacting.

Similarly, a key principle in protecting our relationships is to see clearly what's behind us, our history, and how it is impacting our interactions today. Not using our rearview mirrors is dangerous when we're driving. Denying the impact of the past is equally destructive in relationships because we're more likely to react rather than respond appropriately. When we act inappropriately, we often cause relational whiplash and collisions.

For example, at a small dinner party, my friend teased me about my overreaction to one man's comment at church. She told the others sitting at our table, "We were discussing a particular woman's problems and how we could best support our friend. Her husband had been emotionally and physically abusive to her for years and she was finally at the point of leaving him but did not know how she would support herself financially. One of the men standing there said, 'Well, I think there are things she could be doing to improve her relationship with her husband—then she wouldn't need to be concerned about providing a roof over her head. As they say, love conquers all.'

"That's when Georgia's mouth dropped opened," my friend continued. "She just glared at him. I was sure she was going to jump down his throat."

"You're right," I said. "I thought his comment was thoughtless given the complex and intense situation she was facing. Love is often not enough. Jesus was the epitome of love, and yet the hearts of some people remained hardened. They still held on to their bitterness and hatred." Throwing up my hands, I added, "Oh, let's face it, he's just a typical man thinking it's okay to treat women in such a shallow, unfeeling way."

"Whoa!" both men at our table said in unison.

For a split second I was caught off guard by *their* strong reactions. Then I realized that these two men consistently sought to be caring and respectful to the women in their lives. I was the one who was thoughtless. *My* disrespectful comment, my overreaction, had led to their response.

I cringed. "I'm sorry. Without even realizing it, I put you two and all other men into the same category as my father, who usually treated women with great disrespect."

My father has been dead for forty years, but there are still too many moments when I see other men through that distorted lens I formed as a child. Too easily, I slip back into the old mindset that all men are like my dad and treat women as objects or second-class citizens.

If we remain aware, we can tell when we overreact due to something from our past. Watch for inappropriate emotional displays such as excessive yelling, withdrawing, criticizing harshly, or, in my case, commenting sarcastically. In contrast, when we respond appropriately, we usually do so in a way that shows emotional control and a "proper respect to everyone" (1 Peter 2:17).

It is never too late to stop reacting and start learning how to respond appropriately. Once you acknowledge the impact of the past, you'll be able to gain clarity on how your current connections are shaped by your history. You'll more clearly see the lens you formed growing up, the hurts that haven't healed, and the skills you haven't learned. You'll also be in a position to make conscious choices about current inter-actions rather than automatically reacting.

The Lens You Formed Growing Up

During the first year Kristen was married to Graham, he did not wash their car. Not once. Month after month she wondered why but never mentioned it to him. She also was aware that Graham never thought to trim the straggly bushes in the front of their home.

Growing more and more resentful, Kristen finally asked one night at dinner, "Is there any particular reason why you haven't washed our car?"

Graham looked surprised. "I don't know. I guess it never occurred to me." He looked down at his plate, paused, and looked up again. "Actually, I was wondering why *you* haven't washed it. My mom always washed our cars growing up."

"Did your mom also trim the shrubbery?"

"Yeah. Why?"

"Because at my home my father always washed the cars and my father trimmed the bushes." She smiled. "Isn't it interesting that we've both been waiting for the other person to do those jobs?"

Our expectations of others are influenced by the lens we formed growing up. If a boy was catered to by his mother and she picked up his dirty clothes and towels, then right or wrong, when he becomes a husband he will expect his wife to do the same. If a woman's father always balanced the checkbook, she'll expect her husband to do the same. Whether it's a relatively small matter like who washes the car or a huge thing like the desire for a certain financial standard, the past influences all of us.

Marissa was an only child who was adored by her father. Sitting across the table from me at a women's luncheon, she wore a trendy black jacket with a black-and-white polka-dotted silk scarf. "I truly was Daddy's little princess," she said. "I could do no wrong. My closet was filled with the latest fashions, and Daddy bought me a BMW convertible for my sixteenth birthday.

"When I met my husband, Aiden, I knew he had little money. He even told me when he proposed that he could not afford to support my lifestyle. But I loved him and I was sure we would be fine.

"Lately, however, I'm depressed, and we argue most of the time about money. He says he feels lots of pressure from me to be a better provider. Even my best friend told me I don't realize how much I've come to expect a certain lifestyle. I want to make it work with Aiden, but I like having nice things. I don't know what to do."

No longer blinded to the fact she prefers the lifestyle her father provided, Marissa faces a choice. She can either let go of her material wants or continue to be resentful and burden Aiden with her unrealistic expectations. Her choice may well make or break her marriage.

The Hurts that Haven't Healed

Recently, during a trip to the local mall with a friend, we crossed paths with a woman whom I'll call Teresa. I'd met her years ago.

"My life sure has changed since I last saw you," Teresa said. "Five years ago I divorced the most conniving deceitful person you'll ever meet." She pointed her index finger close to my face. "He was as handsome as they come, but the jerk managed to steal almost all my money and make my life miserable."

For the next ten minutes we were held captive by Teresa's poisonous monologue describing every detail of how her ex-husband had taken advantage of her. He had been a womanizer and used her money to take several of the women he was unfaithful with on exotic trips. Then Teresa glanced at her watch. "Need to run but I just want you to know that the wounds of betrayal were deep but I've decided the heck with him, I'm moving on with my life. I hope one of these days I'll find a nice guy."

As we walked into the next store I glanced at my friend. She looked just like I felt—like Teresa had just vomited all over us. I said, "You look as drained and exhausted as I feel."

My friend nodded. "How's she ever going to move on with all that bitterness and resentment? She's fueled by her anger."

"You know, I honestly believe she has no idea the caustic effect she just had on us."

You might be wondering why so many people are clueless about their unhealed wounds. Why do they fail to see what is in plain sight and obvious to the rest of us? We usually have clarity about how others still carry issues from their past, but we remain fuzzy about our own. To overcome that fuzziness, we need the ability to see areas where we have been blinded by our past. Whether God uses an honest person, something we read, or the Holy Spirit, He is able to point out the tender spot or gaping wound that still needs His healing touch.

The Skills We Haven't Learned

Even when we do recognize the hurts that haven't healed, many of us lack the skills needed to care for our wounds. When Diane, whom I met at a conference, reflected on her past, she was able to see how her sadness as a child was displayed as anger and rage. "I didn't know what else to do with it. I never learned how to handle my frustrations, sadness, or disappointments in a positive way," Diane said, "I was just one angry kid. Later, when I got married, I'd often explode whenever my husband upset me." She smiled. "I finally learned how to get sad rather than mad. For example, recently my husband hurt my feelings. In the past I would have been furious. Now I'm able to say to him, 'What you said hurt me. I'm sad, not mad.'"

Her eyes sparkled. "The beautiful thing was he heard me and then we both could safely talk about the incident without blaming each other." Diane's clarity about her past has enabled her to learn how to respond more appropriately in the present and as a result her relationship with her husband is growing deeper.

Maybe you haven't learned to grieve. Grieving means giving yourself time and space to protest the pain and to feel all your emotions from that loss. You acknowledge to yourself what can no longer be so that eventually, one day, you can accept what now is. You admit to yourself that you wish things were different, but you realize that you cannot go back and change the past.

Perhaps you never learned the skill of forgiving. Forgiveness is a choice we make and a process we work through. Although you may never feel like forgiving, you make the decision to move forward toward freedom as you slowly rid yourself of resentment and find ways to express your anger constructively.

The Insecurities that Are Still Easily Triggered

Author and Christian coach Shannon Ethridge says she helps people learn and understand what's happening in their present by connecting the dots from their past. She asks clients to map out the ten most emotionally stressful and pivotal moments of their lives. "Knowing where the inner turmoil was in the past," Shannon says, "helps people identify what lens they're looking through when viewing other relationships." Here are some key questions Shannon suggests asking yourself about these pivotal moments and your emotions: When do you recall feeling this way as a child? What was your response to this emotion back then? Could you be repeating the same behaviors now for lack of a better strategy?

Maybe one pivotal stressful time for you was your parents' divorce. Maybe it was in junior high when you weren't invited to a party hosted by the popular girl. Both of these experiences can spawn all kinds of insecurities.

Kelly, a woman in her forties, was trying to figure out why she kept sabotaging her romantic relationships. She said she felt too "clingy" and feared "needing" people. A "pivotal moments" discussion with Shannon revealed that Kelly's parents divorced when she was in the first grade, and her mother surrendered custody. Kelly remembers sadly sitting by the living room window, waiting for her mother to pick her up for the weekend, but she often never came. This left Kelly feeling rejected, neglected, and unworthy—which was exactly the same lens through which she often viewed her dating relationships, especially in those moments while waiting for her date to arrive. Because she expected rejection and neglect, that's exactly what she often received. And the way she coped as a child, steeling herself against ever needing anyone too much, tended to be the way she also coped now as an adult.

Once you recognize your insecurities, you can use that knowledge to challenge your self-doubts and the lies that usually accompany them. What are some Scriptures that drive home God's truth? Who can pray with you and help you to reprogram what you erroneously came to believe? What quote, phrase, or statement can you put on your refrigerator, mirror, in your journal, or on your computer to help you realign your thinking? What positive picture or image helps you to counteract the negativity?

Clarissa also has plenty of relational insecurities, especially when it comes to men. "My father left me and my mother when I was four, and I questioned whether I was worthy of being loved for years," Clarissa said. "But instead of being controlled by this lie, I've made the choice to replace it with God's truth that nothing I do can separate me from God's love."

We are all insecure to some degree—we think we are not pretty enough, not smart enough, not rich enough, not thin enough. What creates the real problem, though, is when we fail to notice all the ways our inadequacies hinder our ability to relate to others.

A place of insecurity for me as a teenager was the issue of a clean home. One day I invited a friend to come home with me after school and stay overnight. She not only declined the invitation but turned up her nose and added, "No one wants to stay at your house because it's so dirty."

Although my friend was correct in her assessment of my home during that time, she didn't understand how hard I had worked to clean the house and how insecure I already felt in this area. Having things clean and tidy simply wasn't a priority for my parents. To this day I can experience undue anxiety when my home isn't neat and tidy. But it's an insecurity I am aware of and therefore I am less apt to allow it to impact my relationships in a negative way.

Correct Use of Your Rearview Mirror to the Past

The value of recognizing how the past influences us today is not so we can blame others or feel guilty ourselves. It's not for overanalyzing why we are where we are. Instead, we can use this awareness to learn more about ourselves and how we can best interact with others. We also want a clear perspective so we can minimize our reactions that give those around us relational whiplash.

The first thing we need to do is stop judging ourselves and start learning from the past. We need to change the channel in our mind, so to speak, from the Judging channel to the Learning channel. In her book *Change Your Questions, Change Your Life*, Marilee Adams, Ph.D., discusses the difference between the judger and the learner mindset. Instead of judging ourselves or others and asking questions such as, "What's wrong with me? Whose fault is it? How can I prove I'm right?" (judger mindset), we can choose to ask questions like, "What are the facts? What can I learn? What are my choices?" (learner mindset). [1]

In the learner mindset you're not stuck in the past blaming yourself or anyone one else. Instead, you're making the choice to focus on solutions. You are choosing to learn rather than judge.

For instance, Kyla's divorced mother suffered from manic depression and alcoholism. As a result, her mother could not keep a job and was unable to provide sufficient food for her three children. "When we got hungry," Kyla told me, "my sister, brother, and I would steal empty soda bottles from the back porches of neighbors and return them to the store for cash. We used that money to buy candy so we wouldn't be hungry."

Eventually her mother became so abusive that Kyla's father and his new wife were given custody of the three children. Kyla remained estranged from her mother well into adulthood.

Years later, when she discovered her mother was terminally ill, she and her siblings flew to Texas to visit her. During their brief stay, Kyla often asked her sister questions like, "What are we eating for breakfast?" "When are we going to have lunch?" "Where are we eating dinner?"

After several days of these anxiety-filled questions, Kyla's sister grew frustrated and finally asked, "Why do you keep asking about food? You're not starving, and we can figure out where, what, and when we'll eat as we go."

"When my sister asked me that question," Kyla said, "I realized that being around my mother had stirred up all those feelings and memories of being hungry. Although I have plenty of money to buy myself food, my sister helped me to see what was going on and why I was flooded with anxiety. Now I can understand what was underneath my distress. I was overreacting to my hunger pangs."

Notice Kyla did not wonder, "What's wrong with me?" Nor did she put the blame on her mother and her alcoholism. Conscious awareness of her history enabled Kyla to see what was happening and how she could best contain her anxiety. Like Kyla, you too have a history and some unpleasant memories. Like her, you too can learn from them and gain greater insight in how best to handle them in your daily life.

Years ago, when I was in driver's training, I sometimes failed to respond in a safe manner even when I had a clear view of what was behind me. "Learn from your mistakes," my instructor would say. "How will you respond differently next time?"

You have a history. Learn from it. Use it to check if relational trouble is bearing down on you. If you do happen to overreact to someone, ask yourself, "How can I respond differently next time?" Don't forget that to safely and successfully move forward and avoid those relational collisions, you'll always need a clear view of what's behind you.

STOP: Proceed with Caution

1. What are the lenses you formed growing up that influence your expectations of others?

2. Are there any hurts you haven't acknowledged and allowed to heal?

3. What insecurities do you have? How do you think your past caused those to form and grow?

4. Has anyone suggested that you are easily hurt or offended by a particular type of comment, action, or behavior?

5. Look closely at any strained or broken relationships you have. Are you carrying any mindsets from your past that are hindering your ability to connect with others? We'll discuss solutions for moving beyond these things in the next chapter.

9

I Don't Recognize My Self-Sabotaging Mindsets

Think different thoughts, do different things.

Kim Avery

Traffic jams are incredibly frustrating. The last time I was caught in one I was on my way to the airport to catch an early morning flight. As the freeway traffic slowed from forty miles per hour to ten and then stopped, I could feel my shoulders tighten. Ten minutes later I was still sitting at the same spot, watching the clock and feeling helpless to change my circumstances.

Since I didn't have a GPS device, I decided to phone a friend with my current location. "Assuming I can get to the next exit," I asked, "is there another way to get to the airport? I'm getting desperate."

He gave me directions. After another fifteen minutes of waiting, I made it to the next exit. Thankfully I was able to bypass the heavy traffic and arrive at the airport with enough time to catch my flight.

Similar to being in a traffic jam, many people get caught in self-sabotaging mindsets. They can't move forward and they waste lots of time and energy because they fail to consider other ways of looking at their situation. When I talk about a mindset, I am referring to a fixed way of thinking about something—ourselves, others, or a task. Mindsets are similar to assumptions or stereotypes. We get locked into a certain viewpoint instead of seeing different options and possibilities. Mindsets can be positive and helpful or they can be limiting.

Here's an example of how Addison, an exhausted young mother of two children, was trapped in a self-sabotaging way of looking at parenting. She told me, "My husband and I are both so task-oriented that we don't do the fun things like we used to."

"What were some of the fun things you enjoyed doing?" I asked.

"We loved to go on long hikes and we enjoyed running together. But now we don't give ourselves permission to do those things."

As Addison talked, she shared how her desires to be an excellent parent meant she needed to stop having fun. "My parents instilled in me a strong work ethic. I was taught that having fun was irresponsible. To my mom, fun was bad," she said. "Now that I'm a mom, there is always something that needs to be done for the children and there is no time for me or my husband."

"You talked earlier about being exhausted most of the time. What tends to recharge or re-energize you?" I asked.

"Doing something physical."

"Like going for a long hike or running?"

She smiled.

As we talked, Addison realized she had been unaware that her "work first and only play if there is any time" mindset was keeping her trapped in what she referred to as "a mundane life."

Since she was feeling down about being a mother and her current thinking wasn't getting her where she wanted to be, we explored other ways of looking at what it means to be a responsible parent. At one point I suggested, "Maybe another way of looking at parenting is that responsible moms and dads take care of the necessary tasks and they also carve out time to rest and recharge. Since you both are task-oriented, you could look at making time to have fun and nurture your relationship with your husband as an important task on your to-do list."

Addison agreed. She decided she would give herself permission to have a date with her husband. When I talked to her later, I inquired about the date.

"Well," she said, "habits die hard." Then she laughed. "I asked my husband if we could drop off a gift for a friend. He was quick to remind me that this was our fun time, so we didn't. We went to a state park and ran on one of the trails. It was awesome. We've committed to having a date every two weeks."

For Addison, recharging and building a deeper connection with her husband meant giving herself permission to redefine what it meant to be an excellent parent. Staying stuck in her mindset—a mature and responsible wife and mom takes care of the needs and wants of her family and only relaxes or recharges if there is time left over—was not serving her or her marriage well.

Like Addison, we often don't recognize the thought patterns that can sabotage our relationships. To overcome this relational mistake of not recognizing self-defeating mindsets, you want to identify your negative thoughts and learn to replace them.

Positive and Negative Mindsets

The mindsets you hold are often influenced by your parents, teachers, or significant people in your life. You have also been influenced by the culture in which you live. Up until now, you have probably believed certain things about yourself that you have never questioned. Learning to recognize your various mindsets is the first step toward changing them.

Here is an example of a helpful mindset learned in childhood. Sara Blakely, the billionaire founder of Spanx, said, "My dad encouraged us to fail. Growing up, he would ask us what we failed at that week. If we didn't have something, he would be disappointed. It changed my mindset at an early age that failure is not the outcome, failure is not trying. Don't be afraid to fail."

Sara's father's expectations helped her develop the mindset that failure is not something to be feared. This perspective, in turn, enabled her to take calculated risks which ultimately put her on a successful career track.

Sometimes mindsets are caught rather than taught, and often those mindsets are negative and unhelpful. Emily picked up her perfectionist ways from her father. "Even now, years later as an adult, I've continued to put unnecessary pressure on myself. If something did not go the way I thought it should, I would become frustrated and angry, blame someone, or be critical of myself," Emily said. "Now that I've become more self-aware and recognize what I'm thinking, I'm working toward breaking out of that negative perfectionist cycle."

One of the things that has been especially helpful for Emily is a mentor who points out when she is being especially condemning of herself. "Now I do what I can. I do my best and then tell myself that's enough. Before I always told myself that what I did was not enough. I had very high expectations of how something should be done.

"Of course, anytime I start being hard on myself," Emily said, "I end up depressed. I understand now more than ever how my distorted thinking affects my moods, my behaviors, and my relationships, starting with God. I have so much more freedom these days. My heavenly Father knows I'm not perfect. He does not expect me to be. He accepts me exactly as I am."

Examples of Self-Sabotaging Mindsets

Self-defeating ways of thinking keep us stuck, deplete us of vital resources, and negatively affect our attitudes. It's these self-limiting mindsets, the habitual thoughts and unchallenged beliefs that we want to recognize and replace. But that is often easier said than done. Let me explain four unproductive mindsets and different ways of thinking about them.

Mindset #1: I Don't Have What It Takes

If an important person like a teacher, husband, or sister has treated you as if you have little value and worth, it's easy to continue to carry this perspective without thinking about it.

Tiffany believed she was stupid. She said, "It's easy to think that when your parents and teachers communicated that in thousands of ways." Growing up, Tiffany had a few developmental delays, but she learned to compensate for her disabilities. Even though she had grown into a capable intelligent woman, her self-defeating mindset was holding her back. Slowly, however, through the help of her best friend, Tiffany recognized the lie she had come to believe.

"Thinking I wasn't smart enough to achieve anything had become a well-ingrained habit," Tiffany said. "Even though I could clearly see how my need for affirmation was negatively affecting my relationships, I was still resistant to let it go."

Through her friend and a Bible study group, Tiffany successfully began to challenge her negative view of herself. "It was a real struggle to accept how God sees me but Scripture so clearly mirrors it back to me."

Tiffany said, "I'm beginning to have a healthier view of myself. I'm definitely less needy for the constant encouragement of my friends." And I'm sure Tiffany's friends enjoy being around her more because they don't have to be so careful to be overly complimentary or to treat her differently from the rest of the friends in the group.

Mindset #2: I Can't Move on as Fast as Everyone Tells Me I Should

Grieving is one of those experiences where we can feel and believe we are stuck in our thinking, but in truth we are right where we need to be. The length of time it takes to work through feelings of loss is different for each of us. There is no correct length of time. Whether you are grieving a death, loss of opportunity, a poor choice, or a broken relationship, you can't make a fresh start and be present in all your relationships until you first work through the heartache. Attempting to keep a tight control on your emotions only consumes emotional energy that would be better used on what matters most—acknowledging and working through your feelings.

While in the short term it's easier to ignore the pain, grieving requires time. Time to be. Time to heal. Time to renew your depleted resources. Time to let go of what no longer can be.

Instead of beating yourself up because you're still grieving a loss, consider that it could mean something is *right* about you. When you understand that six to eighteen months after a loss can be the most difficult period, then you'll realize that it's normal to feel worse, rather than better, a year later.

Grief can be intense and debilitating, but failing to grieve means we remain stuck in our pain. Here are a few tips to move beyond the pain to real change.

- Don't resist the grief. Rather, cooperate with it. Give yourself permission to grieve, be willing to say "no" to all but the most important activities. Allow time to cry, reflect, write, or talk through your thoughts and feelings.

- Remember we are only equipped to handle pain in small doses. This is why grieving usually takes longer than we expect or have the patience for. Carve out brief respites in the midst of the difficult times. Instead of trying to deal with the intense feelings all at once, take time to do something that gives you joy or a sense of relief.

- Expect setbacks. Whether it is the smell of cologne, seeing a photo, or hearing a song, just when you think the time of grief is behind you, something may trigger more sadness. Tell yourself that is okay.

Mindset #3: She Doesn't Deserve My Forgiveness

You may be right that this person is not remorseful and doesn't deserve your forgiveness; however, that is not the issue. By holding on to your grudges and resentments, you will stay stuck and become filled with a bitterness that will seep into all your interactions.

How can you rethink the way you look at forgiveness? One possibility is to see forgiveness as a choice you make and a process you work through. Forgiveness is not a feeling. You make the decision to let go of your right to get revenge because you have been forgiven by God (Matthew 18:21-35). Holding tightly to unforgiveness may make you feel powerful and in control, but there are tremendous benefits to your health and well-being when you let go. As psychiatrist Loren Olson noted, "Those more inclined to pardon the transgressions of others have been found to have lower blood pressure, fewer depressive symptoms and, once they hit late middle age, better overall mental and physical health than those who do not forgive easily."[1]

Like grieving, forgiving is far from easy as you work through all the associated emotions, but it is the only path to healing and freedom. Instead of allowing your anger or hurt to lead to conflict with others, here are a few steps to get you started:

- Don't wait for an apology.

- Verbalize your feelings to someone safe rather than nursing your hurt feelings. Remember how God has forgiven you.

- Understand it's not necessary to forget in order to forgive.

- Understand forgiveness is not a once-and-done deal. There are lots of little acts of forgiveness you will need to make along the way.

Mindset #4: If I Were a Better Christian My Life Would Be Easy

I've heard people say things like, "The more mature I become in my faith, the smoother my life will be" or "If this Christianity thing was real, it would be easier and more natural to spend time with God in prayer and reading the Bible." When their reality does not match their expectations, they become discouraged or disillusioned.

One way of challenging that assumption is to say the opposite is true. Because we are obedient to God and doing what he wants us to do, we might encounter more resistance. As Albert Haase, author and former missionary in China, writes, "The spiritual journey gets more difficult the further along a person travels." [2]

What mindsets do you hold about success, failure, yourself, your body, your relationships, God, and the world? Because your mindsets dictate your choices, take some time not only to become aware of what they are but also to think about other ways of looking at them.

Ways to Recognize Your Mindsets

You may find it difficult to identify your self-defeating perspectives, as they are often well-hidden. If this is the case, ask God to reveal them to you and seek a trustworthy friend to let you know when he or she observes you are stuck in a negative thought pattern. Here are three suggestions for uncovering your self-sabotaging mindsets.

1. Pay Attention to What You're Thinking and Saying

We all express our mindsets in different ways, but if we don't pay attention we won't recognize them. One married woman who was trying to make an abusive situation better on her own said, "I caught myself saying the other day, 'If I give 100 percent to my marriage, then my husband will come to appreciate and respect me.' It hit me—I can give 200 percent but that is not going to guarantee my husband will stop harming me physically and emotionally."

2. Notice How Your Perspectives Blend or Clash with Others

One pastor said, "It wasn't until my son asked me one night, 'Dad, why do we always get the leftovers of your time and energy?' that I recognized I needed to rethink my perspective on what it meant to be a pastor. I had always held tightly to the view that helping other people is more important than doing something for myself. At some point, however, I came to believe that included my family. It wasn't until my son said something that I realized that was my mindset. It worked well when I was single and in seminary but that is no longer true now that I am a husband and father."

3. Be Aware of Your Feelings

Self-defeating mindsets usually deplete you of vital energy. They definitely don't energize you and bring positive feelings like peace and joy.

After Blair dropped out of a Ph.D. program, she struggled with feelings of failure. "It felt like I was paralyzed for two years," she said. "One day, as I was chatting and praying with a friend, she helped me to reframe my futile thinking from 'I failed a Ph.D. program' to 'I completed post-graduate work.' That new mindset is so empowering for me. And my husband was thrilled because as he said, 'You have been moping around for a couple of years about that.'"

Rewrite and Replace Your Self-Sabotaging Mindsets

Like Blair, once you see the implications and the ripple effects of self-sabotaging mindsets, the next step is to rewrite and replace that way of thinking with something more helpful. Because our thoughts determine our choices and behaviors, if we want to have better relationships, we need to change our self-limiting habits. Here are three ways to do that:

1. Self-Reflection

Once you uncover a mindset, ask yourself this question: Is this way of thinking crippling me and hurting my relationships or is it God's best for me?

Such self-reflection will be uncomfortable, as it was with the pastor I mentioned earlier. He would never have questioned his perspective on being a pastor and replaced it with a new way of thinking if his son hadn't taken him to task. As long as he was happily self-deluded, nothing would have changed for his family. His son would have continued to get the leftovers. "For as he thinks in his heart, so is he" (Proverbs 23:7 NKJV).

But once the pastor recognized that his son was right, he had to decide what to do about it. It can take lots of work to rethink, rewrite, and replace a deeply rooted mindset. It's an ongoing process that in many cases takes years. Quite often we need the assistance and feedback of those who have a more objective perspective.

2. Holy Spirit Guidance

Ask the Holy Spirit to guide your thinking. "Let the Spirit renew your thoughts and attitudes. Put on your new nature, created to be like God—truly righteous and holy" (Ephesians 4:23-24 NLT).

Realize that even when we replace a self-defeating mindset with a positive one, it is a challenge to sustain the new pattern of thinking. As pastor and bestselling author John Ortberg notes, "Deep change takes more than willpower. It requires God renewing our minds. It requires surrender." [3]

3. Accountability from Friends

As Addison discovered, habits are not easily broken. She found it helpful to rely on God to give her the right thoughts, but she also asked a close friend to hold her accountable for her new way of thinking about parenting. If you have a close, trustworthy friend who can speak the truth in love, why not ask that person to help you? If you don't have such a person in your life, why not ask God to bring such a person to you?

Growth Versus Fixed Mindsets

Stanford University psychologist Carol Dweck found, after years of research, that there is a huge difference in success when you hold a growth mindset instead of a fixed mindset. As the author of *Mindset: The New Psychology of Success,* she writes, "In a fixed mindset, people believe their basic qualities, like their intelligence or talent, are simply fixed traits. They spend their time documenting their intelligence or talent instead of developing them...In a growth mindset, people believe that their most basic abilities can be developed through dedication and hard work—brains and talent are just the starting point. This view creates a love of learning and a resilience that is essential for great accomplishment." [4]

Because your mindset dictates your choices, take some time to be aware of which ones are getting in your way. Which ones are blocking your progress? Which ones are negatively affecting your relationships?

As you become aware of your mindsets, keep in mind this wise advice:

> Watch your thoughts, they become words.
> Watch your words, they become actions.
> Watch your actions, they become habits.
> Watch your habits, they become your character.
> Watch your character, it becomes your destiny.

While a mindset does take time and effort to replace, be willing to take one small step toward thinking differently.

STOP: **Proceed with Caution**

1. What is one limiting belief you are holding onto that is keeping you stuck in a negative way of relating to someone? If you aren't aware of any, then ask a friend, mentor, or family member for feedback to help you see what you might be missing. Like the pastor, realize that what worked for you in the past might not be helpful in your current circumstances.

2. What mindsets do you hold about God? About being a Christian? Maybe you're thinking that as a Christian you must choose between having fun and following Jesus. Is this scripturally true?

3. Once you become aware of a self-sabotaging mindset, ask yourself if there is another way you can look at it.

10

I Think I'm the Exception to the Rule

Be honest in your evaluation of yourselves.

<small>Romans 12:3 nlt</small>

O ne of my friends tried to educate her husband about the blind spots on the right and left sides of a car's front windshield. She explained to him how it's important for the driver to check the blind spots so he doesn't miss a vehicle or pedestrian. Her attempt to educate him, however, failed. He assured her that, unlike the rest of us, *he* did not have that blind spot.

This story is a wonderful illustration of our tendency to be deceived and somehow think we are the exception to the rule. It's also a great example of how challenging it is for us to listen, be teachable, and humbly hear what others are trying to tell us.

Maybe, like me, you look back on a particular relationship, shake your head, and wonder why you didn't listen to a friend who was honestly trying to help you. Instead, you wonder, *How could I have been so stupid?*

Many years ago I dated a man who was handsome, intelligent, and who I thought was a real gentleman. He enjoyed taking me to lovely restaurants. He was kind and caring to my son, which, as a single mother, was a real plus. I was sure he was the one.

I knew he had a long history of broken relationships but I thought I was different. I really did think I was special somehow.

When some of my closest friends questioned his integrity and character, I thought, "He's not like that anymore. They don't under-stand how much he's changing. Things are different now."

After a couple of years of dating, however, he ended our relation-ship. I was devastated. As I grieved, I was forced to face the truth. I had been blinded to his true character because I thought his feelings for me were different from his affections for the other women he dated. The blind spot of thinking I was the exception caused me months of heart-ache and pain. It was a pain my friends and family had tried to protect me from. It was a hard lesson to learn, but the experience taught me that the sooner I realize and accept that I have more in common with other people than I thought, the wiser my relationship choices will be in the future.

It's not just singles who experience this blind spot and think they are the exception. As brothers or sisters, we often get frustrated if we share what we're seeing in a sibling's relationship but he or she ignores us. We can see our sister headed for heartache—that she really doesn't see the truth about her friend—but no matter how gently we offer our opinion, she refuses to listen and tells us we don't understand.

As parents, we've experienced firsthand how this relational blind spot impacts our sons and daughters. We know our loved ones don't always see people or situations clearly, but they think they can handle it. It's painful to watch a son or daughter develop a relationship with a person or group of people that we believe is not healthy. When we express our concerns, more than likely our children will ignore, rebuff, or contradict the issues we raise. And most likely, because of this rela-tional blind spot, they think it will all turn out well.

This blind spot can also be experienced in our work relationships. We've seen what happens when a coworker doesn't understand how manipulative his or her boss is. We may watch as they trust a coworker who should not be trusted. We try to warn our friend but get nowhere. We may wonder, "Why can't they see what's going on? Why won't they listen to me? How can an intelligent person be so stupid at times?"

We incorrectly assume—too often—that other people's suggestions or experiences really don't apply to us. If we hear something about the average person we ignore it because we usually think we are above average. For instance, studies suggest that the average driver will have a close call every month or so, but most of us don't think that statistic pertains to us. Why? Because most of us consider ourselves to be safer than the average driver.

In his book *Stumbling on Happiness*, Harvard psychologist Daniel Gilbert states, "Science has given us a lot of facts about the average person...one of the most reliable of these facts is that the average person doesn't see [himself or] herself as average."[1]

Remember the cartoon *Yogi Bear*? Yogi was known to say, "I'm smarter than the average bear!" but look what happened to him. Yogi overestimated his cleverness and usually ended up in trouble with Ranger Smith. His poor little sidekick, Boo Boo, was usually heard saying, "But Yogi..." as he unsuccessfully tried to point out what Yogi was not seeing.

Not everyone, however, is like Yogi Bear. Not all of us think we are superior or better than the average bear. Dr. Gilbert says, "In certain areas like computer skills or juggling we might see ourselves as inferior." But whether we consider ourselves superior or inferior "we almost always see ourselves as unique."[2] We think the rules don't apply to us. We can smoke, drink, or take drugs and not become addicted. We can eat too much fat or sugar and our arteries won't become clogged. We can talk or text while driving and not have an accident.

Regardless of whether you have the tendency to underestimate or overestimate yourself, both viewpoints are shortsighted and create relational difficulties.

Overestimating Yourself

Many of us overestimate our abilities. In short, we think too highly of ourselves. Galatians 6:3 tells us, "If anyone thinks they are something when they are not, they deceive themselves." Peter, Jesus's disciple, is a perfect example of how we can think of ourselves too highly. He told Jesus, "Even if all fall away, I will not" (Mark 14:29). Yet we read later in Scripture that Peter repeatedly denied knowing Jesus.

We, like Peter, are weak and flawed. We hold overinflated views of ourselves only to repeatedly stumble and fall. For example, you might misjudge your ability to stay healthy. You tell yourself, "I don't need a flu shot this year." Before the season is over, you might end up with the flu, miss a week of work, and maybe even become too sick to attend a child's important concert.

Another example of overestimating yourself might be you receive a poor evaluation at work and believe it's not about your performance but about your manager's lack of insight. Instead of recognizing that you need to change a few of your work habits, you steadfastly hold on to your perception of your performance and undermine those who are trying to work with you.

When you discount or reject valuable information about your true self, you usually take risks that are not worth taking. And you miss an opportunity to grow in self-awareness and become a better person.

We have all wanted what we want no matter what others tell us, what the wisdom of Scripture says, or the reality of the situation. We are arrogant enough to think things will all turn out well. In the end, we suffer the consequences. The cost is usually paid in our health, in our career, in our relationships with people, and in our relationship with God.

Underestimating Yourself

It's equally shortsighted to focus too much on all your shortcomings and flaws. Kelly told me, "I'm not really good at anything. I don't know if I even fit into God's plan. I know we're called to serve, but I haven't figured out how I can help others." Kelly felt inferior to other Christians. She minimized her strengths and questioned how God could use her.

When you consistently underestimate the gifts God has given you and question His ability to empower you, you miss out on many blessings. The Israelite spies who were sent to explore the Promised Land are a great example of this. Unlike Caleb and Joshua who thought the Israelites could take possession of the Promised Land with God's help, the majority of the spies said, "We can't attack those people; they are stronger than we are…We seemed like grasshoppers in our own eyes, and we looked the same to them" (Numbers 13:31,33).

They spread their fear and disbelief like a deadly virus. Despite Moses's assurances that with God it was possible, the Israelites refused to try. As a result of their disobedience, none of them, except Caleb and Joshua, ever entered the Promised Land.

The Relational Fallout of Thinking We Are the Exception

Thinking we are the exception has a negative impact on us and our relationships. When you have a puffed-up sense of your importance or talents, you can be insensitive and look down on others. You're likely to become easily offended when you don't get the attention you feel you are entitled to. You may be resentful and hold little grudges, thinking, "I spend hours each week doing errands for my husband and he rarely says thank you." In reality, you are probably overestimating your importance and underestimating your husband's contributions.

You may think, "My mother is so unappreciative of all the meals I make for her" or "My boss seldom recognizes all the ways I cover for him in the office." In reality, your mother probably appreciates what you do but she may show her appreciation in ways that you don't notice. And perhaps your boss does know you cover for him, but he doesn't want to say so for fear that he will lose his authority. In both cases, your sense of being an exception, if unchecked, will fester and lead to increasingly negative attitudes and poor behavior on your part.

Those of us with a deflated sense of self often don't reach out or help others for a different reason. We don't think we have anything of value to share. We are guilty of thinking of others too highly *and* thinking about ourselves too much. You might be afraid, for example, to have your friends over for lunch. You're overly concerned that the food won't be perfect or they will judge your home. You don't sign up for that committee at church because you feel too uncomfortable or you're afraid you'll mess things up for others.

One of my friends said, "I often discounted the gifts God gave me because I felt worthless. I didn't realize how wrapped up I was in myself. Now I try to forget about myself. I look around at a group of people and see the people who feel like I did, who feel like they are on the fringe. I purposely reach out to them and try to make them feel welcomed and wanted."

Regardless of whether you have an inflated view of yourself, like Peter, or a deflated view of yourself like the Israelites in the desert, you are not seeing yourself accurately or hearing what others are trying to show you. Worse, you are not seeing God and what He wants you to see.

To protect yourself from thinking you're the exception to the rule, here are three strategies you can follow: recognize your tendency to think you're the exception, cultivate a teachable attitude, and see yourself as uniquely created, but not the exception to the rule.

Recognize Your Tendency to Think You Are the Exception

We rarely have a balanced view of ourselves or see ourselves as we are. We usually aren't as good as we think we are or as bad as we think we are. We aren't as talented as we think we are, nor are we as incompetent as we believe. The truth usually lies in the middle.

Sara served on the worship team and she was a small group leader at her church. "I never said I was more important or more spiritual, but I certainly acted that way." Her exaggerated sense of importance led to more than one broken relationship. "Because I put in so many hours each week at church, I expected my opinions to be of greater value. Of course no one wanted a know-it-all telling them what they should do."

How do you think about or treat people in your life? Do you think of people as stupid or less spiritual or immature? Or do you see others as more capable, more spiritually discerning and wise? What is your underlying attitude? Recognizing you have an inaccurate perception of yourself is the first step toward correcting this flaw.

Cultivate a Teachable Attitude

How teachable are you? How willing are you to hear things about your friends, your abilities, and your choices? Having a teachable spirit goes a long way toward helping you grow in self-awareness.

Melody had heard stories about how vicious her friend Kelsey could be, but Melody never thought anything hurtful would happen to her. She never thought Kelsey would turn on her because she was so interested in what was going on in Melody's life and so willing to lend a hand with the children. But when Kelsey betrayed one of Melody's deepest confidences, Melody realized she wasn't immune to being stabbed in the back by her friend. "What upsets me the most about that experience is my closest friends warned me numerous times. Why did I think this time things with Kelsey would be different when nothing really changed in her? Why wasn't I more open to hearing what they were saying? Next time I will have a totally different attitude and listen to those I love and trust."

These "mirror moments," when you realize something about yourself you never noticed or acknowledged before, are transforming. From that point on you are different because you view yourself in a more accurate way.

Claire and her husband decided to adopt two children because of infertility issues. But Claire still yearned to experience pregnancy. When her sister-in-law became pregnant and she seemed to have no emotional response, either positive or negative, Claire was irritated. One night as she complained for the hundredth time to her husband about what she considered her sister-in-law's poor attitude, he said, "Claire, you need to be careful. You are going to become a very bitter person."

Claire said, "My husband was not a critical person and I knew I needed to take what he said to heart. But my prideful self wanted to resist hearing his suggestions."

When we have a prideful attitude rather than a teachable one, we aren't open to seeing ourselves clearly. A proud person is more interested in giving advice than hearing or taking advice. Proud people like to correct others rather than receive constructive comments and grow. And they certainly aren't as willing to listen or pray about the insights those closest to them have shared.

Noted missionary and author Andrew Murray writes, "Let us… admit that there is nothing so natural to man, nothing so insidious and hidden from our sight, nothing so difficult and dangerous [to our relationships], as pride."[3]

Pride wreaks havoc in our relationships by breeding quarrels, stirring up discord, and causing conflicts. A teachable attitude, however, enables us to at least listen to each other's suggestions and, most impor-tantly, seek God and his counsel. As a result, being teachable brings us blessings:

> Now then, my children, listen to me;
> blessed are those who keep my ways.
> Listen to my instruction and be wise;
> do not disregard it.
> Blessed are those who listen to me,
> watching daily at my doors,
> waiting at my doorway.
> For those who find me find life
> and receive favor from the LORD (Proverbs 8:32-35).

See Yourself as Unique, Not as the Exception

Anthropologist Margaret Mead said it this way, "Always remember that you are absolutely unique. Just like everyone else."

One area that particularly suffers when we think we are an excep-tion is our relationship with God. It's not uncommon to hear people say, "God loves everyone but me. I've made too many mistakes. I'm too broken." Their erroneous beliefs about being an exception keep them feeling far from God.

Maybe you believe God forgives everyone but you, or, that he can use and empower everyone but you. Bella said, "I never believed what God said about our value was meant for me. I never felt worthy. But one year our Bible study teacher gave each one of us a jar filled with personalized verses and suggested we read one each day. Day after day I would read those verses with my name in them. Finally one morning it hit me—I'm special too. God is speaking to me, Bella."

Maybe you tend to have a more puffed-up view of yourself. Here's one example of how you can see yourself more accurately. William Beebe, the naturalist, told about visits that he made to the home of Theodore Roosevelt, who also enjoyed nature. Beebe writes, "After an evening of talk, perhaps about the fringes of knowledge, or some new possibility of climbing inside the minds and senses of animals, we would go out on the lawn, where we took turns at an amusing little astronomical rite. We searched until we found, with or without glasses, the faint, heavenly spot of light mist beyond the lower left-hand corner of the Great Square of Pegasus, when one or the other of us would then recite: 'That is the Spiral Galaxy in Andromeda. It is as large as our Milky Way. It is one of a hundred million galaxies. It is 750,000 light-years away. It consists of one hundred billion suns, each larger than our sun.' After an interval Colonel Roosevelt would grin at me and say: 'Now I think we are small enough! Let's go to bed.'" [4]

At the beginning of this chapter, I shared how my friend's husband was sure he did not have a blind spot on either side of his windshield. He was sure he and his vehicle were exceptions to the rule. A few days later, however, he arrived home quite shaken and admitted he had come very close to causing a crash. "I almost hit a small car. I didn't see it until the last second," he said.

It turns out the vehicle was hidden by the right frame of his front windshield. "I guess you were right," he told my friend. "I really do have that blind spot after all."

You are unique and God created you like no other. But, as Paul suggests, "Don't cherish exaggerated ideas of yourself or your importance, but try to have a sane estimate of your capabilities" (Romans 12:3 PHILLIPS).

STOP: Proceed with Caution

1. Was there a time when you thought other people's experiences or suggestions really didn't apply to you?

2. How open are you to listening to the advice of people you respect and trust? Are you inviting feedback from others to help you grow in self-awareness?

3. How has your better-than or less-than attitude created problems in a relationship?

11

I Allow My Strengths to Become Weaknesses

Every personal strength when overused has the potential of becoming a personal weakness.

CLAUDIA M. SHELTON

My friends each have their own styles of driving. Those with a more laid-back personality are usually not in any hurry and don't seem to care if others pass them on the road. While driving, they like to poke along and enjoy the scenery, not realizing their speed has slowed. While I appreciate their relaxed easygoing nature, I can get frustrated and annoyed when we tarry too long and arrive late to a special event, like a surprise birthday party.

My goal-oriented friends, on the other hand, drive more aggressively and travel the most direct and efficient route possible. Sometimes, however, I feel that reaching the destination is far more important to them than their interest in connecting and interacting with me along the way.

My friends who have an outgoing personality love to share their latest stories while they drive. They talk, sometimes using both hands. They frequently look at me instead of the road ahead, and I sometimes feel like they only want to talk, rather than listen to any experiences I may want to share.

My organized, perfectionist friends have planned out the trip in detail, complete with TripTik and reservations. It can be stressful riding with them, however, when their perfect plans get thrown off by a detour in the road or an exceptionally long traffic jam. Being flexible and going with the flow can be a challenge for them.

Understanding the diversity of our friends, their personalities, their strengths, and their weaknesses is important. Each personality type has strengths that, when taken to extreme, become weaknesses.

For example, I'm the kind of person who loves to set and achieve goals. This is a strength that enables me to complete many tasks and projects. If I am not paying attention, however, I can become too focused on my goals and neglect the people in my life. Although I may *want* to see myself as a motivated and productive person, I need to be aware that my family or friends might have a totally different perception. They may, in certain situations, see me as driven and uncaring.

Another example is someone who is very creative and spontaneous. They may accurately see themselves as having the ability to take the most mundane day and turn it into an adventure. They may remain unaware, however, that others perceive them as irresponsible, trying to use their creativity to wiggle out of any boring task.

Identify Your Personality

To see yourself and your interactions objectively, you want to understand your personality type and gain a realistic view of how any strength can become a weakness. There are more than fifty personality inventories on the market today. You may have taken one of the many personality assessments, such as the Myers-Briggs Type Indicator® or DISC® profile. For the purposes of seeing our blind spots, I am going to use one developed by Marita and Florence Littauer to help you understand how you are wired. They label four basic personality types: Popular Sanguine, Perfect Melancholy, Powerful Choleric, and Peaceful Phlegmatic.[1]

Popular Sanguine

The Popular Sanguine is the high energy, outgoing person who loves to talk, tell stories, and make people laugh. Their basic desire in life is to have fun. They are spontaneous and creative, often thinking out loud by bouncing ideas off others. The Popular Sanguine has great people skills and can quickly bring a group of strangers together. We often find them using their warmth and energy to greet partygoers or conference attendees.

Perfect Melancholy

The total opposite of the Popular Sanguine is the detailed, sensitive, perfectionistic Perfect Melancholy. They desire organization and perfection. The Perfect Melancholy is attentive to detail and a gifted planner. They love structure, appreciate outlines, and enjoy breaking a process into smaller steps. When expressing their thoughts or feelings, Perfect Melancholies are deliberate in their thinking. They are also sensitive and compassionate. They listen with their hearts, having the ability to sense what is going on beneath the surface.

Powerful Choleric

The Powerful Choleric can focus on goals and achieve them. They are get-it-done kinds of people. This personality is the natural-born leader and willing to take on challenges some of the other personalities want to run from. Their basic desire is for control and their style of communicating is direct and to the point.

Peaceful Phlegmatic

The Peaceful Phlegmatic is the relaxed, easygoing person who everyone likes. They enjoy peace and quiet. Even constructive conflict is difficult for them as they don't like to make waves. The Peaceful Phlegmatic values and respects people and brings a sense of calm into the most chaotic situations. They tend to watch what is going on around them, pondering issues before expressing their thoughts or feelings.

None of these four personalities is better than another. All have a unique set of strengths and weaknesses. Most of us are a mixture of at least two types. For example, you might be a blend of the Powerful Choleric and the Popular Sanguine whereas your daughter could have the Perfect Melancholy and Peaceful Phlegmatic personalities. It would make for an even more interesting household if your husband was also a Choleric Melancholy and your son was a Phlegmatic Sanguine.

If you are having trouble identifying your personality, reflect on which personality feels more comfortable for you. Which one best describes your natural, shoes-off self? If you are still clueless, ask several people who know you well to tell you which of the personalities they think best describes you.

Understand the Link between Your Strengths and Weaknesses

Because communication is such a key part of our relationships, we'll focus on the strengths and weaknesses of the different personalities along with their styles of interacting. Since we are all capable of rationalizing and justifying our behaviors, our goal in this chapter is to gain a more accurate view of the positive and negative influences our personality can have on others. When we see ourselves clearly, we are more aware of the changes we can make to improve our relationships.

Strengths and Weaknesses of Popular Sanguine

My friend Betsy, a Popular Sanguine, is a warm, inviting person who seems to know everyone. Some of her Popular Sanguine traits are spontaneity, creativity, and charm. Betsy is outgoing and a great storyteller. These wonderful traits, however, can become weaknesses in the following examples.

First, spontaneous and creative comments can be funny or hurtful. Popular Sanguines are quick on their feet. I'm always amazed at the ideas or comments Betsy comes up with—just like that. For example, I can be slaving over a title for an article and she'll come up with a brilliant idea in a split second. The danger is that at times, especially in conversations, she reacts too quickly. She sometimes speaks before she thinks, saying the first thing that comes to her mind. While it may be funny to the group, it may be at the expense of someone's feelings. She has had to learn to first filter her thoughts by asking herself, "Is what I'm about to say hurtful or helpful?"

Second, outgoing and charming people can talk with anyone or monopolize conversations. The Popular Sanguine is gifted at making people feel comfortable and welcome. But my friend Betsy will tell you if she isn't paying attention she can talk incessantly, not realizing how much she is dominating a conversation. She said, "I can lose sight of the ways it becomes all about me." Even though she hates pauses in conversations, she's working on getting more comfortable with open spaces and giving others the opportunity to talk. "It's amazing what happens when I catch my breath and create an open space in a conversation," Betsy told me. She monitors herself by asking, "Am I giving others a chance to speak?"

Third, great storytellers can add entertainment or get off topic. It's fun to hear Betsy share her latest experiences. But she's learned that no matter how great the story, if it doesn't fit with the topic being discussed or the point she is trying to make, it needs to be saved for another time. She's self-aware enough to realize that not everyone wants to be constantly entertained. "Since I always have plenty of stories, I try to make it a game and decide which story is best for the conversation," she says.

Be aware, that when you, a Popular Sanguine, are stressed you tend to talk constantly or talk too loudly, make sarcastic or cutting remarks, and have problems focusing your thoughts and comments.

Strengths and Weaknesses of the Perfect Melancholy

The Perfect Melancholy is the total opposite of the Popular Sanguine. We are the thinkers. We like to mull things through. I say "we" because this is one of my personality types. Even communicating through social media is not easy or natural for us. I can't just throw something out on Facebook; I have to think about it first.

If this is your personality, your strengths are attending to details, planning and organizing, and being sensitive and compassionate; but these, too, can become weaknesses when carried to the extreme.

First, those who give attention to detail can be helpful or obsessive. You understand facts and figures and can help others see what is critical to completing a project. Carried to an extreme, however, you can bog others down with all the minutiae. Learn to prioritize, communicating only the most important details to others. Creating self-awareness means asking questions like, "Am I sharing too many facts and figures?"

Second, gifted planners and organizers can be precise and critical or too rigid. As a communicator and coach with this personality, I enjoy bridging the gap from where someone is right now to where they want to go. On the other hand, I can become paralyzed, especially under pressure, believing that there is only one perfect way to do something. I can also become critical, rigid, and inflexible, thinking my way is the perfect way. Self-awareness for me is realizing that not everyone is, or wants to be, as organized as I am. I need to take the time to reflect and ask myself, "Am I holding on to my perfect plan too tightly?"

Third, sensitive and compassionate people can be perceptive or hypersensitive. If you are a Perfect Melancholy, you are sensitive to the feelings and struggles of others. The danger is your sensitive spirit can become easily offended. You may sense something is going on under the surface but you can interpret its meaning incorrectly. For example, you know your coworker is upset, but you think he is irritated with you when in fact he is angry with his wife. Self-aware people with this personality are willing to ask themselves, "Am I being too sensitive? Am I overanalyzing and making incorrect assumptions about what is really going on?"

When stressed, especially over a long period of time, the Perfect Melancholy can become paralyzed, inflexible, and unable to see the big picture. They might avoid people or situations they can't straighten out and criticize the behavior of others.

Strengths and Weaknesses of the Powerful Choleric

This natural-born leader can set a goal and focus on it until she achieves it. Powerful Cholerics don't give up easily. They are get-it-done people. If this is your personality, you are a gifted leader and don't quickly back down from a challenge. But too much of a good thing can be your downfall.

First, gifted leaders can provide direction or overpower. Powerful Cholerics have the tendency to think they know what should be done, who should do it, and how it should be done. One of my friends bought her Powerful Choleric husband a T-shirt that said, "Things will go more smoothly if you'll just admit I'm right."

While they are often right in their assessments, they can perceive their opinions as the truth—which may or may not be accurate. They may also be seen as bossy and offend others. People may start to resent, become passive-aggressive, procrastinate, or sabotage the work just to show the Powerful Choleric who really is in charge.

If you have this personality, seeing yourself objectively means asking yourself, "Is this just my opinion or is it really the truth?"

Second, people who love challenges can fix things but ignore feelings. The Powerful Choleric is capable of dealing with difficult situations. They are often able to say the hard things that no one else wants to say. The challenge is to remember you can't solve every problem and some people don't need fixing.

For instance, one Powerful Choleric told me how she tries to support her mother who is the primary caregiver for her terminally ill father. My friend said, "I am always trying to fix things for her, telling her, 'Here's what you need to do.'" Aware of her tendency to do this, my friend said, "I need to remember that sometimes it is far better to listen and let my mother talk."

Challenge yourself by asking, "Am I trying to fix something that can't or doesn't need to be fixed?"

Third, focusing on goals is productive but can be insensitive and cold. The Powerful Choleric can make things happen and they don't like to waste time doing it. Your challenge is to make sure you don't allow your goals to become more important than the people in your life.

My son and I both have powerful personalities. Several months ago he called me looking for corporate sponsors for the college swim team he coaches. He got right to the point of asking if I had any suggestions of whom he could contact without even saying, "Hello, how are you doing, Mom?" When I failed to think of anyone he could contact, he was ready to hang up and move on. Without knowledge of his personality and style of communication, I could have been hurt and offended.

While your tendency, like my son, might be to focus on the goal, remember that the most effective way to get the results you want is through people and relationships.

Even though you may see chatting with someone as a waste of time, often these informal interactions will help you uncover valuable information or enable you to encourage another person. By building your relationships, you will be more apt to get the results you want when you later need to call on someone to help.

Being self-aware means asking, "Have I allowed my goals to become more important than the people in my life?"

When stressed, the Powerful Choleric often becomes bossy, demanding, or irritated. She has little tolerance for mistakes or honest errors.

Strengths and Weaknesses of the Peaceful Phlegmatic Personality

This personality type is laid-back and easygoing. They don't like to make waves and are more than happy to stay in the background, providing an audience for the other personalities. However, you and those around you may lose your peace if your strengths aren't held in check.

First, relaxed and easygoing people can be calm or check out. You are gentle, balanced, and bring a soothing touch into many of your conversations. The challenge for you is not only to watch what is going on around you but to be willing to expend energy. Get involved in the conversation or activity. Even though you may be hesitant to contribute, thinking no one needs to hear from you, take the risk to express your thoughts and perspectives.

In a Bible study group I attended years ago, one of the peaceful personalities rarely contributed any comments because she said, "I don't feel like I have anything valuable to contribute." Self-awareness for this personality is to realize that people are often left guessing what you are thinking and feeling. Ask yourself, "Am I actively interacting and engaging with others?"

Second, cooperative spirits can either mediate or fail to deal with conflict. The Peaceful Phlegmatic is gifted at compromising when necessary, since they know how destructive conflict can be. On the other hand, they may ignore issues that need to be faced or confronted because of their desire to keep the peace. They need to consider that doing the hard things in the short term makes it easier for them later on.

Megan, a Peaceful Phlegmatic, said that when her son and her husband are upset and yell at one another, "It's like someone rubbing coarse sandpaper on my skin. It makes me feel really bad. I prefer to avoid conflict and disagreement at all costs. Even if it means pushing things under the rug, I would rather see someone happy."

If you are a Peaceful Phlegmatic and don't speak up, people may have the tendency to ignore you, which may lead to feelings of resentment on your part. Ask, "What issues have I avoided that I need to deal with? What thoughts, feelings, and opinions do I need to express?"

Third, Peaceful Phlegmatics can either work well under pressure or withdraw. One of my friends who has this personality is the supervisor of a nursing staff. During an emergency she quietly comes in, deals with the issue, and then moves on to the next crisis. However, she realizes she can't wait until things are falling apart in her personal relationships before she becomes involved. In personal matters she routinely asks herself, "Am I waiting for a crisis, or am I willing to get involved now?"

When stressed, Peaceful Phlegmatics tend to swallow feelings and give in just to keep the peace. They consistently shut down during conflict and may become withdrawn from conversation.

Regardless of your personality, gaining an objective view of your strengths is critical for understanding yourself. Equally important is tempering those strengths so they don't become detrimental to your relationships. While the Popular Sanguine brings energy and enthusiasm to their relationships, they will have to guard against talking too much and blurting out hurtful comments. The Powerful Choleric brings intensity and focus but needs to be mindful of the thoughts and feelings of others. The Perfect Melancholy provides the depth and the details as long as they don't get obsessive and demand perfection. The Peaceful Phlegmatic adds the gift of calm but needs to learn to confront when necessary and express themselves rather than withdraw.

When it comes to our personalities, we are all self-deceived to some degree. What if, by growing in self-awareness and gaining a realistic view of your strengths, you could minimize the number of misunderstandings with family or friends? What if you could reduce some of the miscommunications you have with your boss or coworkers? How would your relationships be different if you could express yourself in a way that maximizes your strengths and minimizes your weaknesses? Are you ready to find out?

STOP: **Proceed with Caution**

1. What is your personality and basic desire? Do you want to have fun, be in control, have things organized and perfect, or just have peace and quiet?

2. What are the strengths of your personality?

3. How are you intentionally using your strengths to serve others?

4. In order to temper your strengths so they don't hinder your relationships, list one or two questions you can routinely ask yourself.

12

I Lose Sight of the Big Picture

We are limited, not by our abilities, but by our vision.

KAHLIL GIBRAN

The term "inattentional blindness" refers to our failure to notice a person or object that is in full view because our attention is focused on something else. This relatively new term was coined in 1992 by Arien Mack and Irvin Rock, professors of psychology at Berkeley.

Professors Mack and Rock explain it this way: "Most people have the impression that they simply see what is there and do so merely by opening their eyes and looking."[1] But researchers have found that we miss things that are right in front of us. We not only fail to notice things but we're clueless to the fact we missed them. Illusionists use inattentional blindness all the time. They are gifted at getting us to focus our attention elsewhere while they perform their tricks.

A demonstration of inattentional blindness can be found online if you search "invisible gorilla video." In this study, completed at Harvard University, there are two teams playing basketball, one team with white shirts and the other with black shirts. Your instructions, while watching the video, are to count the number of passes the white team makes. As the teams are passing the ball, a person in a black gorilla suit slowly walks among the players. Researchers found that "half of the people who watched the video and counted the passes missed the gorilla. It was as if the gorilla were invisible."[2]

In the same way as the students who focused on the number of passes and missed the gorilla, whatever we focus on is what we see. It's as if we're blind to everything but one spot. Here's one example of what happens in our relationships when we focus only on a few things or on the *wrong* things.

One of my single friends, Andrea, went on a blind date. This was arranged by her married friend, Jillian, who raved about how handsome and friendly this man was.

Within the first twenty minutes of their date, Andrea discovered that this man had been divorced three times, had just filed the papers for bankruptcy, and was addicted to gambling.

Andrea, who has two jobs and little free time, told me, "I was extremely upset that Jillian would even think I would want to spend one of my precious free evenings with this guy. As soon as I arrived home from that date, I called Jillian and asked her what she was thinking! Why would she even remotely think I would be interested in dating this man for any length of time?"

Jillian, who obviously failed to see the whole picture, said, "But he's really handsome and friendly."

When we become fixated on the wrong things—in this case good looks—it can lead to misunderstandings in our relationships. We can use this knowledge about inattentional blindness, however, to empower ourselves. When we understand this relational mistake—losing sight of the big picture—we can protect ourselves by consistently focusing on the most significant things, knowing the insignificant things will fade away.

In the movie *The Weather Man*, the main character, played by Nicolas Cage, shows what happens when we fail to attend to what's most important to us: We one day find ourselves far from where we wanted to be. In a final scene, Nicolas Cage is walking on a dreary city street as he reflects back on his life. He says, "I remember once…imagining what my life would be like, what I'd be like. I pictured having all these qualities. Strong, positive qualities…that people could pick up on from across a room. But as time passed…few ever became any qualities I actually had. And all the possibilities I faced, and the sorts of people I could be…all of them got reduced every year to fewer and fewer…until finally they got reduced to one…to who I am. And that's who I am…the weather man."

What will your life and your relationships look like years from now? Unless you know what strong character qualities you want in your life and remain focused on developing them, you will not be the person you want to be.

Author Stephen Covey encourages us to live with the end in mind. "To begin with the end in mind means to start with a clear understanding of your destination. It means to know where you're going so that you better understand where you are now and so that the steps you take are always in the right direction…We may be very busy, we may be very efficient, but we will also be truly effective only when we begin with the end in mind."[3]

Gwen is a mother of four children, and she has done an excellent job of living with the end in mind. She and her husband have four children, two of whom are adopted and have severe disabilities. In a home of six people, things can get pretty crazy. Gwen told me, "Even when things are nuts and I'm exhausted, I constantly remind myself of the big picture. I focus on God and how He can use these experiences to develop my character and make me stronger. Otherwise I think I would give up. Being a good parent is important to me. Family, compassion, and loving relationships are three of my core values. I believe God is using these difficult times to equip me to help others."

One of Gwen's dreams is to one day finish the book she is writing on tools and strategies for children with a specific learning disability. Instead of losing sight of the big picture, Gwen keeps her sanity by routinely centering her attention on the most important issues. Like Gwen, when you keep a clear view on the most significant issues, the less significant ones that threaten to consume you naturally fade into the background. But it is a process you may have to repeat over and over again.

Your Values

Failing to identify and remain centered on your values is an all-too-common occurrence. Your values shape your life and influence all the decisions you make. Have you ever taken the time to consider what values are most important to you? Do you have clarity on what your priorities are?

As part of my training to become a life coach years ago, I had to identify my top five core values. I didn't think the exercise was important and completed the assignment only because it was required. Over the years, however, I've come to realize how critical this self-knowledge is. You will be more likely to make wise choices if you consider your values *before* making major decisions, such as accepting a new job or getting into a relationship.

My top five values are my commitment to Christ, family, integrity, excellence, and beauty. Before I clarified that beauty is very important to me, I tended to ignore that part of myself. I would tell myself things like "Gardening is wonderful, but flowers are frivolous. I should grow something useful like tomatoes or asparagus." When I recognized that beauty gives me joy, feeds my soul, and is also important to God, I willingly embraced it as one of my top five values.

Family is another one of my top five values. If I choose that value, I periodically need to consider how my life reflects that fact. If my time, energy, and resources are being consumed by my friends and a career, I need to either reprioritize my schedule or consider that family really isn't as important to me as I said it was.

To help you get started on clarifying what is most important to you, go to the appendix on page 163. As you complete the exercise, ask yourself this: Do my actions, calendar, and checkbook reflect the values I say are most important to me?

In our relationships, it's important to understand how our values align with the people we live and work with. Are our values in conflict or compatible with theirs? For example, one of your core values may be stability. You treasure a lifestyle with little change or upheaval. In contrast, your spouse holds dear the value of adventure. He loves new and thrilling experiences. When not identified, these opposing values are responsible for many misunderstandings and disagreements.

While our values don't need to be identical with others, it is going to be a much more harmonious relationship when they are compatible. In a serious dating relationship, it's critical to identify each other's values. Not for the purpose of trying to change another person, but so that you can clearly see the big picture of how compatible you are. If faith is number one to you and it isn't even on the top-ten list for the person you are dating, you have to ask yourself if you want to commit to marriage and raising children with that person in the future.

Remember, a blind spot is either something we don't see or something we notice but *discount*. Don't minimize the significance of clashing or colliding values. When you understand that your values define you, you'll see the importance of accepting differences in values without giving up yours.

Married couples often don't realize their values don't align until they begin raising children, and these value clashes can be the source of recurring arguments. One spouse may value adventure while the other values safety. The partner who values adventure will expose the children to all sorts of challenges and excitement, while the other will be aghast that a good parent would ever consider allowing, much less encouraging, children to do such things. Having a big heap of respect for one another is necessary. Both adventure and safety are good. A good parent will observe clues that each child gives about what types of things he or she values. One child may thrive in adventurous surroundings while another child in the same family may require large doses of peaceful security.

Your Dreams

When my son was still living at home, he and I often discussed our dreams and which ones were currently impossible for us—things that only God could do. One of Kyle's dreams was to get a full college scholarship in swimming. Each morning before he got on the school bus, we diligently prayed for those dreams. Those prayers not only helped us to keep a clear view of our dreams, but they also reminded us how much we needed God's help in achieving them.

There were lots of struggles along the way. Kyle did not swim half of his junior year of high school because of medical problems and was sick his senior year with mononucleosis. In spite of the setbacks, however, Kyle did his part by working hard and holding on to the dream.

But ultimately we knew it was something only God could have done—Kyle received a full college swim scholarship based on his swim times from tenth grade.

Recently I realized that somehow over the last decade, since Kyle left home, I had forgotten most of my dreams. As I reflected on this gradual change over the years, I wondered how I, a person who once had such bold dreams, became someone with so few. My dreams slowly disappeared because of inattentional blindness. Instead of focusing on them, I neglected my dreams and allowed them to fade away.

When you no longer pay attention to your dreams, you lose a passionate and valuable part of who God created you to be. I'm thankful that a few months ago, during a personal retreat, my most cherished God-given dreams resurfaced, along with my passion and joy. Once again I have a clear view of them and once again I'm excited to watch how God brings them to fruition. I don't need to know how I'm going to do this. If God called me, he will equip and guide me.

Instead of giving so much attention to all the reasons you'll never reach your dreams, focus on the desires burning deep within your heart. Receive the dream God has for you. Have the courage to live the dream by doing the hard work and "though it linger, wait for it" (Habakkuk 2:3). As Oswald Chambers writes, "Every hope or dream of the human mind will be fulfilled if it is noble and of God. But one of the greatest stresses in life is the stress of waiting for God." [4]

Be Attentive to the Important

We know from the research on inattentional blindness that what we attend to gets noticed and what we don't focus on gets lost in the busyness of life. How can you be attentive to what is most important to you? I have found three strategies that can help you to stay focused on the big picture. Slow the pace of your life, be accountable, and record your values and dreams.

Slow the Pace of Your Life

Recently, a number of my appointments were cancelled and I gained one whole day where my calendar was clear. As I leisurely went from one task to the next, I noticed how the frantic pace of my life had made me lose sight of the big picture. During that day I was more mindful of God's hand in my life, more open to hearing what He wanted to tell me, and more attentive to what he wanted me to see. Since I wasn't racing from one task to the next, I also found myself listening more carefully to what those closest to me were trying to communicate.

At the end of that unexpected slow-paced day, I realized how I'm paying less attention to what I value. Because of this tendency to drift away from what's most important to me, I've found it helpful to have someone keep me accountable.

Be Accountable

Being accountable to someone is helpful for keeping the main things the main things. While you may resist setting up some kind of structure, realize you can't go it alone. Whether you choose to have an accountability partner, a coach, a counselor, or a mentor, or join a small group, you need the encouragement and support of at least one other person.

When I asked one woman how she was doing staying focused on her dream of publishing a book, she said, "Well, I sorta forgot all about it. And I guess my friend who said she'd hold me accountable did too. She never asked me if I was staying on track." Do not assume that just anyone will be a good accountability partner. Pick someone who is task-oriented and not afraid to confront you in a loving way. Unless you pick someone reliable, the chances of getting derailed are pretty high.

Record Your Values and Dreams

Whether you record your values, dreams, and goals in a journal or on the computer, write them somewhere you can easily retrieve them. Once a week refresh your memory by rereading your values and dreams. You need those values firmly planted in your mind if you are going to live them. Ask yourself, "How am I doing in living my values? Am I drifting away from them?"

Michael Hyatt, author and former CEO of Thomas Nelson Publishers, shared the story of a difficult time at his company. He went on a personal retreat. After much prayer, he created a new vision for his staff. He wrote, "I personally read through this vision daily. I prayed over every part. I asked God to guide us. Little by little, He brought us the strategy and the resources. However, I spent way more time—probably ten-to-one—focused on the *what* rather than the *how*."[5]

Keeping the *what*, the big picture, in sight is essential. Otherwise, we will become bogged down by the little stuff. If you want to be a better parent, grandparent, or coworker, what specifically would you like to do? Would you like to have face time with your granddaughter once a week? Do you want to spend five minutes each day focusing only on your daughter? Do you want to take your married son out to lunch once a month? Would you like to be more attentive to the needs and struggles of your coworkers? If so, keep the goal in mind by writing it down and reflecting on it daily.

Knowing you can't pay attention to everything, begin now to separate what's important from what's not. Doing so will give you a clarity that you never had before. All too often we wait for a crisis or some tragic loss before we remember to look at our values and our big dreams. Readjust your priorities so you can hold onto your newly gained insights. Whether you want to spend more time with your family and friends, become less competitive, or not let the little things stress you as quickly, routinely take the time to slow down, revisit, and pay attention to what's most important to you. Become accountable to live your values and make your dreams a reality. Live your life on purpose, guided by God's plan rather than by the daily distractions of life.

STOP: Proceed with Caution

1. How would you rate yourself on paying attention to what you say is most important to you? Name one step you can take toward being more focused.

2. Are you clear about your top five values? If not, take the time needed to clarify them.

3. Do you understand what values are most important to the people you live and work with? Try to identify a couple of their values and then have a discussion with them about this topic.

4. How compatible are their top five values with yours? In what ways do they clash? How can you be respectful and honoring of each other's values without losing your own?

Vision for Life

The wise are cautious and avoid danger;
fools plunge ahead with reckless confidence.

PROVERBS 14:16 NLT

Misunderstandings. Conflicts. Damaged friendships. Destroyed marriages. We've all endured the hurts and complexities of relationships. On the other hand, when we do experience deep meaningful connections, we feel invigorated and fulfilled. Since we know relationships are vital to our well-being, how can we, as flawed humans relating to other imperfect people, enjoy the stronger, healthier relationships we yearn for?

While we can't control how others treat us, one way we can improve our emotional connections is by choosing to reduce and avoid some of the hurt and pain we cause others. Just as we routinely check our mirrors as we drive, we routinely must learn to be attentive to our relational blind spots. Both behaviors require continual practice if we want them to become the good habits they should be. Here are four steps you can take to increase your self-awareness.

Accept Your Tendency for Self-Deception

We can't banish blind spots, but we can learn to compensate for them by first recognizing and accepting our tendency to be deceived. As author and pastor John Ortberg writes, "We are all viewing ourselves in the fun house mirror…That is why we are often stunned when someone else sees past our defenses into our souls. It is not that they are geniuses. It is just that I am sitting right in my blind spot." [1]

We have to pay attention to our amazing ability to make excuses, shift the blame, or justify our poor choices. Jesus called the Pharisees blind because they were so focused on their behaviors that they did not see the state of their hearts. Like the Pharisees, we also can miss what's in our hearts if we don't look past our self-delusions. As Dr. Madeleine Van Hecke writes in *Blind Spots: Why Smart People Do Dumb Things*, "Our minds work for us in wonderful ways—80 or 90 percent of the time. But the rest of the time, functioning in the very same ways, our minds work against us."[2]

Heeding the Warnings

Have you ever noticed that large trucks often have a warning reminding you of a potentially dangerous situation? One notice I recently saw said, "If you can't see my mirrors I can't see you." These warnings are put in a conspicuous place for our safety and should not be ignored.

Growing in self-awareness is an ongoing process. Just as it's dangerous to drive without paying attention to our visual blind spots, it's equally hazardous to go through life without paying attention to the ways we can get trapped in our perceptions.

Self-awareness is not something we naturally possess. A two-year-old child is self-centered but not self-aware. Self-awareness is something that must be cultivated if it is to develop its full potential as you grow and mature. Carve out time for self-examination, not so you can become self-absorbed, but so you can get a clear picture of who you are—your warts and blemishes, your skills and talents, your need of God's forgiveness, and God's wonderful gifts of mercy and grace to you.

Use Your Mirrors

In some of his final thoughts to Timothy, the apostle Paul instructs him to use his mirrors. Well, he doesn't say it quite that way. He says it this way: "Watch your life and doctrine closely" (1 Timothy 4:16). Just like we need mirrors to see the dirt on our face, we need the mirrors of truth-tellers, Scripture, and the Holy Spirit to help us gain insight into who we really are and what needs to change.

Truth-tellers

Because perception problems lead to people problems, we need to seek the counsel of wise, trustworthy people who are able to speak the truth in love. We need at least one person who will hold us accountable and point out what we fail to see. While it is distressing to think about someone seeing and knowing all our inner ugliness, pride, and greed, we need to remember that God already sees it and loves us anyway. The sooner we identify a trustworthy person and ask that person to help us, the sooner we will be on our way toward positive change.

Scripture

Reading Scripture daily is a great habit as it reminds us of the truth which is so easily forgotten. Memorizing Scripture is also helpful. But meditating on the Word of God day and night really helps counteract the distorted thinking we have about ourselves and God. Scripture can correct inaccuracies we have come to believe and enable us to see things from God's perspective.

Holy Spirit

Recently, as the morning light flooded my bedroom window, I noticed dust on my furniture and dirt on my carpet that I hadn't seen earlier. The dust and dirt had been there, but I hadn't noticed it because of the dim light. When we allow the light of God's Spirit to shine truth into our hearts and minds, we will see personal sin and long-forgotten grime that we never noticed before. We will feel uncomfortable. But persevere. Ask the Holy Spirit to cleanse you and show you how and where to make changes. Beware: He will do as you ask.

Make Necessary Adjustments

Once you gain insight into your blind spots, you need to make changes to remove what is hindering your ability to connect with others. Real change and growth comes when you stop ignoring your flaws.

Use the questions and suggestions listed throughout this book to move beyond the darkness of your self-deceptions into the light of self-awareness. It is my prayer that in your relationships, you will project God's light, rather than darkness, onto others.

As painful as your relationships may be now and as hard as it is to sustain the effort to change, it is worth it. In order to S.P.O.T. what you may not see, remember to...

Seek God's wisdom

Pause for clarity

Open yourself up to wise counsel

Take a step back to gain a new perspective

If you do so, you'll experience deeper, more meaningful connections. Your life and relationships will become exponentially richer. And isn't that a vision worth working for?

What's Most Important to You? 40 Value Questions

Our values shape our lives and impact the decisions we make. To help you get started on clarifying what is most important to you, listed below are forty values with related questions. This is by no means a complete list of all possible values. Begin by reading over the list and choose ten values. Put those aside for a few days or weeks and observe how you make decisions. After a time of reflection, narrow your list to five core values that best represent what's most important to you. One word of caution about identifying your core values: Sometimes what you may identify at first as being very important to you might not end up being a key value. Give yourself plenty of time. It's not unusual for the process of determining your top values to take weeks or months.

Generosity	Loving Relationships
Do you regularly give a part of your income to those in need, a church, or an organization?	Do you enjoy spending your time, energy, and resources on others?
Adventure	**Beauty**
Do you appreciate new and thrilling experiences?	Do you cherish God's creation and the beautiful things in life?
Humor	**Authenticity**
Do you love to laugh and see the lighter side of things?	Do you value saying and doing what is true to who you are?

Compassion
Do you appreciate tenderness, kindness, and sensitivity to the needs of others?

Knowledge
Do you set a high value on learning and contributing information?

Commitment to Christ
Do you cherish a relationship with Jesus and follow Christian principles?

Excellence
Do you enjoy doing something to the best of your ability?

Fame
Do you enjoy being recognized and known by other people?

Financial Responsibility
Do you value living within your means, saving, and paying your bills on time?

Fun
Do you love to be playful, entertain others, and clown around?

Service
Do you enjoy helping others?

Power
Do you value influence and control?

Integrity
Do you consistently strive to follow your standards of what you perceive to be right, honest, and just?

Joy
Do you delight in a cheerful, sunny disposition?

Peace
Do you cherish times of tranquility without conflict or chaos?

Family
Do you enjoy a close, loving family that spends time together?

Respect
Do you value, accept, and honor others?

Stability
Do you treasure a balanced life with little change or upheaval?

Security
Do you appreciate freedom from danger or worry?

Spirituality
Do you value the spiritual aspects of life?

Achievements
Do you enjoy accomplishments and making things happen?

Trust
Do you appreciate people who are reliable and keep their word?

Career
Do you highly esteem your work or profession?

Wealth
Do you love to have an abundance of money, possessions, and/or property?

Wisdom
Do you set a high value on being discerning, wise, or insightful?

Challenge
Do you enjoy solving demanding or difficult problems?

Independence
Do you like to be free from reliance on others?

Fitness
Do you like to be physically strong and in shape?

Cooperation
Do you value working with others as a team?

Adaptability
Do you appreciate the ability to be flexible and adjust to changing circumstances with ease?

Humility
Do you like to be modest, unassuming, or unpretentious?

Justice
Do you feel strongly about fair and impartial treatment for all?

Loyalty
Do you highly value people who are faithful?

Leisure
Do you treasure time to relax and do what you want?

Ambition
Do you value hard work and the drive for advancement?

Order
Do you value neatness with everything in its assigned place?

Solitude
Do you enjoy having the time and space to be alone?

Notes

Introduction

1. Carol Tavris and Elliot Aronson, *Mistakes Were Made (But Not by Me)* (New York: Harcourt, 2007), 42.

2. Ibid.

3. Henry T. Blackaby and Claude V. King, *Experiencing God: Knowing and Doing the Will of God* (Nashville, TN: Lifeway Press, 1990), 77.

4. Henri Nouwen, *In the Name of Jesus* (New York: Crossroad Publishing, 1989), 13.

5. Oswald Chambers, *My Utmost for His Highest* (Grand Rapids, MI: Discovery House Publishers, 1992), March 28.

6. Madeleine L. Van Hecke, *Blind Spots* (Amherst, NY: Prometheus Books, 2007), 37.

7. Ibid.

8. Tavris and Aronson, *Mistakes Were Made*, 192.

9. Mark Batterson, *The Circle Maker* (Grand Rapids, MI: Zondervan, 2011), 129.

Chapter 1

1. Travis Bradberry and Jean Greaves, *Emotional Intelligence 2.0* (San Diego: TalentSmart, 2009), 26.

2. Albert Haase, O.F.M., *Coming Home to Your True Self* (Downers Grove, IL: IVP Books, 2008), 72-74.

3. Henri Nouwen, *A Cry for Mercy: Prayers from the Genesee* (New York: An Image Book, 2002), Monday, February 19.

4. Pat Lencioni, *Getting Naked: A Business Fable About Shedding the Three Fears That Sabotage Client Loyalty* (San Francisco: Jossey-Bass, 2010), 214.

5. Pam Farrel, "Fine-Tuning Friends," *Just Between Us*, Spring 2011, 28.

Chapter 2

1. Ruth Haley Barton, *Strengthening the Soul of Your Leadership* (Downers Grove, IL: IVP Books 2008), 104.

2. Richard Swenson, *Margin: Restoring Emotional, Physical, Financial and Time Reserves to Overloaded Lives* (Colorado Springs, CO: NavPress 2004), 27.

3. Barton, *Strengthening the Soul of Your Leadership*.

4. Jim Loehr and Tony Schwartz, *The Power of Full Engagement* (New York: Free Press, 2003), 29-30.

5. Oswald Chambers, *My Utmost for His Highest* (Grand Rapids, MI: Discovery House Publishers, 1992), April 13.

6. Swenson, *Margin*, 69.

7. Tom Rath and Jim Harter, *Wellbeing: The Five Essential Elements*, (New York: Gallup Press, 2010), 9.

8. Chrissie Grace, "The Captivity of Activity," *In His Grace* (blog), March 9, 2010, http://chris siegrace.blogspot.com/2010/03/captivity-of-activity.html.

9. Kim Caviness, "Eat, Pray, Roll Camera!" *WebMD*, July/August 2010, 16.

Chapter 3

1. Albert Haase, O.F.M., *Coming Home to Your True Self* (Downers Grove, IL: IVP Books 2008), 30.

2. Oswald Chambers, *My Utmost for His Highest* (Grand Rapids, MI: Discovery House Publishers, 1992), August 7.

Chapter 4

1. Zoë B, "How Neuroplasticity Can Increase Your Intelligence," *Simple Life Strategies,* March 24, 2012, http://simplelifestrategies.com/sls-neuroplasticity-jilltaylor/.

2. Leslie Vernick, in personal correspondence with the author.

3. Daniel Goleman, *Social Intelligence* (New York: Bantam Books, 2006), 5.

4. Ibid., 13.

5. Ibid., 318.

6. Leslie Vernick, *Emotionally Destructive Relationships* (Eugene, OR: Harvest House Publishers, 2007), 26.

7. John Ortberg, *The Me I Want to Be* (Grand Rapids, MI: Zondervan, 2010), 206.

8. Henri Nouwen, *Bread for the Journey* (San Francisco: HarperOne, 1997), May 1.

9. Robert D. Putnam, *Bowling Alone: The Collapse and Revival of American Community*, (New York: Simon & Schuster, 2000), 332.

Chapter 5

1. Tim Sanders, *The Likeability Factor* (New York: Three Rivers Press, 2006), 117.

2. John Townsend, *Beyond Boundaries* (Grand Rapids, MI: Zondervan, 2011), 87.

3. Carol Tavris and Elliot Aronson, *Mistakes Were Made (But Not by Me)* (New York: Harcourt, 2007), 10.

4. Judy Smith, interview, *The Today Show,* NBC, March 1, 2013.

5. Jennifer Goodwin, "Malpractice Suits Drop When Doctors Admit Mistakes, Apologize," *USA Today,* August 20, 2010, http://usatoday30.usatoday.com/yourlife/health/healthcare/doctorsnurses/2010-08-20-medical-errors-malpractice_N.htm.

6. Tavris and Aronson, *Mistakes Were Made,* 219.

7. Ibid., 180.

Chapter 6

1. Albert Haase, O.F.M., *Coming Home to Your True Self* (Downers Grove, IL: IVP Books, 2008), 48.

2. Daniel Goleman, *Vital Lies, Simple Truths: The Psychology of Self-Deception* (New York: Simon & Schuster, 1985), 39.

3. Ibid., 243.

4. Gregory Karp, "Cash vs. Credit Mindset," *Chicago Tribune News*, December 15, 2011, http://

articles.chicagotribune.com/2011-12-15/news/sc-cons-1215-karpspend-20111210_1_credit-cards-card-balances-debit-cards.

5. Henry Cloud, "The Pruning Influence," *Christian Counseling Today* 1, no. 3 (2012).

6. Haase, *Coming Home to Your True Self,* 50.

7. Jeff Manion, *The Land Between* (Grand Rapids, MI: Zondervan, 2010), 192-93.

Chapter 7

1. Travis Bradberry and Jean Greaves, *Emotional Intelligence 2.0* (San Diego, CA: TalentSmart, 2009), 6.

2. Daniel Goleman, *Emotional Intelligence* (New York: Bantam Books, 1995).

3. Bradberry and Greaves, *Emotional Intelligence 2.0*, 13.

4. Leslie Vernick, newsletter, February 7, 2012, http://www.leslievernick.com/newsletter/020712-newsletter.html.

Chapter 8

1. Marilee Adams, *Change Your Questions, Change Your Life* (San Francisco: Berrett-Koehler Publishers, Inc., 2009).

Chapter 9

1. Loren Olson, "Forgiveness: Your Life Depends Upon It," *Family Therapy Magazine* 10, no. 2 (March/April 2011): 28-31.

2. Albert Haase, O.F.M., *Coming Home to Your True Self* (Downers Grove, IL: IVP Books, 2008), 152.

3. John Ortberg, *The Me I Want to Be* (Grand Rapids, MI: Zondervan, 2010), 65.

4. Carol Dweck, "What Is Mindset," *Mindset,* accessed July 25, 2013, http://www.mindsetonline.com/whatisit/about/index.html.

Chapter 10

1. Daniel Gilbert, *Stumbling on Happiness* (New York: Alfred A. Knopf, 2006).

2. Ibid., 229.

3. Andrew Murray, *Humility* (New Kensington, PA: Whitaker House, 1982), 19.

4. William Beebe, ed., *The Book of Naturalists* (Princeton, NJ: Alfred A. Knopf, 1944), 234.

Chapter 11

1. Marita Littauer, *Wired That Way* (Ventura, CA: Regal Books, 2006).

Chapter 12

1. Arien Mack and Irvin Rock, *Inattentional Blindness* (Cambridge, Massachusetts: MIT Press), 1998, 1.

2. Christopher Chabris and Daniel Simmons, "Gorilla Experiment," *The Invisible Gorilla,* 2010, http://www.theinvisiblegorilla.com/gorilla_experiment.html.

3. Stephen Covey, *The 7 Habits of Highly Effective People* (New York: Fireside, 1989), 98.

4. Oswald Chambers, *My Utmost for His Highest* (Grand Rapids, MI: Discovery House Publishers, 1992), February 22.

5. Michael Hyatt, "Why Vision Is More Important than Strategy," *Michael Hyatt: Intentional Leadership*, January 23, 2012, http://michaelhyatt.com/why-vision-is-more-important-than-strategy.html.

Conclusion

1. John Ortberg, *The Me I Want To Be* (Grand Rapids, MI: Zondervan, 2010), 157.

2. Madeleine L. Van Hecke, *Blind Spots* (Amherst , NY: Prometheus Books; 2007), 20.

About the Author

Georgia Shaffer is a licensed psychologist in Pennsylvania and a certified life coach. She is a regular columnist in *Christian Coaching Today* and a board member of the International Christian Coaching Association. She is also an instructor with the American Association of Christian Counselor's Professional Coaching DVD Series. With more than twelve years of coaching experience, Georgia specializes in life coaching for women, relationship coaching, coaching the coach, and coaching for authors and speakers.

She is the author of *Taking Out Your Emotional Trash: Face Your Feelings and Build Healthy Relationships, A Gift of Mourning Glories: Restoring Your Life After Loss,* and *Twelve Smart Choices to Finding the Right Guy,* which will be released in 2014. In her book *Coaching the Coach,* Georgia compiled stories and tips from more than 45 leaders in Christian coaching.

Georgia speaks frequently at professional conferences, women's retreats, and singles' and cancer survivor events, helping people identify answers to the questions, "What needs to grow? What needs to go?" in their life and relationships.

Georgia has also appeared on television shows such as *The 700 Club, The Sharron and Hermann Show, Decision Today,* Sky Angel's *A Time for Hope,* and on the DVD *Jesus: Fact or Fiction?*

When she isn't writing, speaking, or coaching, Georgia enjoys spending time with her friends and family and gardening.

For additional resources, check out:
www.GeorgiaShaffer.com

Taking Out Your Emotional Trash
Face Your Feelings and Build Healthy Relationships
By Georgia Shaffer

What needs to grow and what needs to go? Licensed psychologist and author Georgia Shaffer asks women this vital question as she encourages them to recognize and let go of the unhealthy, toxic emotions and lies they hold onto and replace them with godly truths.

With a strong biblical foundation, Shaffer offers encouragement, insightful questions, practical steps, and personal prayers to help readers

- release destructive guilt and insecurities by embracing their value in God
- reduce anxiety by addressing their deepest fears with God's wisdom
- experience greater intimacy and honesty in their relationships
- increase their physical energy and spiritual peace in God's strength
- turn from unrealistic expectations toward realistic expectations and positive goals

Readers will discover hope and renewal as they watch God transform their trash into treasure through His mighty grace.